SPECIAL-DAY CALENDAR CARDS

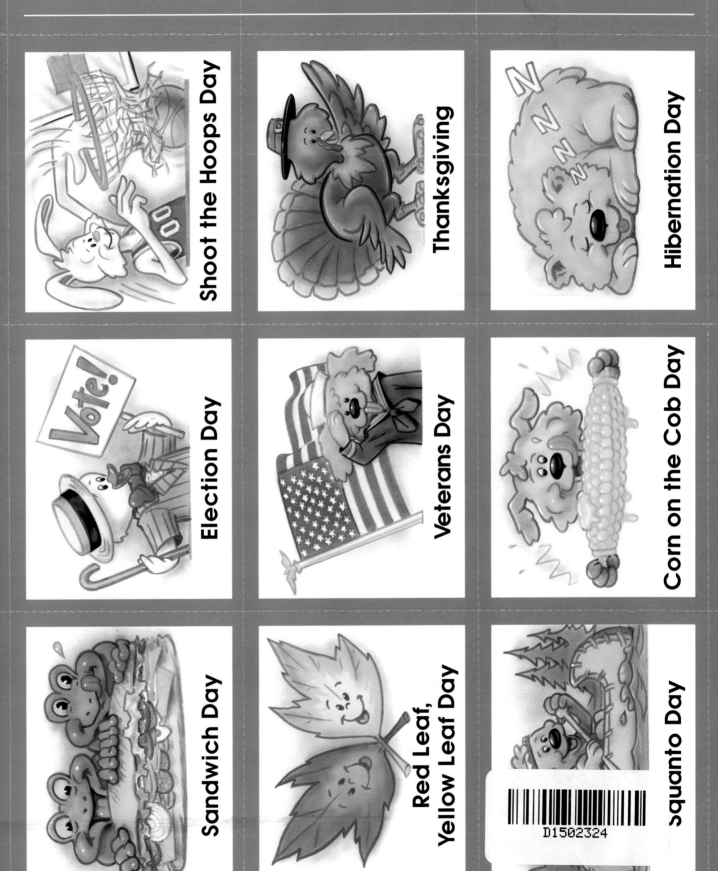

SPECIAL-DAY CALENDAR CARDS

Marvelous Maps Day

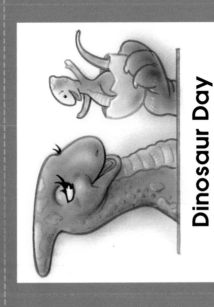

Dinosaur Day

Quilt Day

Peanut Butter Day

Happy Birthday!

We Hooray for Arthur!

ARTHUR BY MARC BROWN

Arthur Day

Airplane Day

Celebrate the Months
NOVEMBER

EDITOR:

Kristine Johnson

ILLUSTRATORS:

Darcy Tom

Jane Yamada

PROJECT DIRECTOR:

Carolea Williams

CONTRIBUTING WRITERS:

Trisha Callella   Kimberly Jordano

Rosa Drew   Mary Kurth

Marguerite Duke   Terry Petersen

Ronda Howley

TABLE OF CONTENTS

INTRODUCTION

Seasons, holidays, annual events, and just-for-fun monthly themes provide fitting frameworks for learning! Celebrate November and its special days with these exciting and unique activities. This activity book of integrated curriculum ideas includes the following:

MONTHLY CELEBRATION THEMES

▲ **monthly celebration activities** that relate to monthlong and weeklong events or themes, such as Fabulous Fall Feasts, Family Week, and Terrific Turkeys.

▲ **literature lists** of fiction and nonfiction books for each monthly celebration.

▲ **bulletin-board displays** that can be used for seasonal decoration and interactive learning-center fun.

▲ **take-home activities** that reinforce what is being taught in school, encourage home–school communication, and help children connect home and school learning.

SPECIAL-DAY THEMES

▲ **special-day activities** that relate to 15 special November days, including Thanksgiving, Election Day, and Dinosaur Day. Activities integrate art, songs and chants, language arts, math, science, and social studies.

▲ **calendar cards** that complement each of the special days and add some extra seasonal fun to your daily calendar time.

▲ **literature lists** of fiction and nonfiction books for each special day.

FUN FORMS

▲ a **blank monthly calendar** for writing lesson plans, dates to remember, special events, book titles, new words, and incentives, or for math and calendar activities.

▲ **seasonal border pages** that add eye-catching appeal to parent notes, homework assignments, letters, certificates, announcements, and bulletins.

▲ a **seasonal journal page** for students to share thoughts, feelings, stories, or experiences. Reproduce and bind several pages for individual journals, or combine single, completed journal pages to make a class book.

▲ a **classroom newsletter** for students to report current classroom events and share illustrations, comics, stories, or poems. Reproduce and send completed newsletters home to keep families informed and involved.

▲ **clip art** to add a seasonal flair to bulletin boards, class projects, charts, and parent notes.

SPECIAL-DAY CALENDAR CARD ACTIVITIES

Below are a variety of ways to introduce special-day calendar cards into your curriculum.

PATTERNING

During daily calendar time, use one of these patterning activities to reinforce students' math skills.

▲ Use special-day calendar cards and your own calendar markers to create a pattern for the month, such as regular day, regular day, special day.

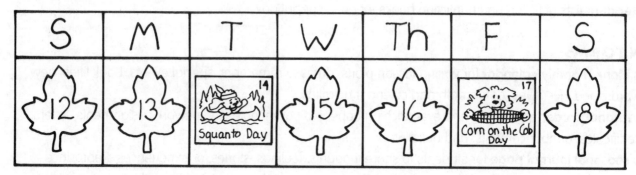

▲ Number special-day cards in advance. Use only even- or odd-numbered special days for patterning. (Create your own "special days" with the blank calendar cards.) Use your own calendar markers to create the other half of the pattern.

▲ At the beginning of the month, attach the special-day cards to the calendar. Use your own calendar markers for patterning. When a special day arrives, invite a student to remove the special-day card and replace it with your calendar marker to continue the pattern.

HIDE AND FIND

On the first day of the month, hide numbered special-day cards around the classroom. Invite students to find them and bring them to the calendar area. Have a student volunteer hang each card in the correct calendar space as you explain the card's significance.

A FESTIVE INTRODUCTION

On the first day of the month, display numbered special-day cards in a festive setting, such as a cornucopia display. Invite students, one at a time, to remove a card and attach it to the calendar as you explain its significance.

POCKET-CHART SENTENCE STRIPS

Have the class dictate a sentence to correspond with each special-day card. Write the sentences on individual sentence strips. For example, on Election Day you might write *On this special day, we vote in elections.* Put the sentence strips away. When a special day arrives, place the corresponding strip in a pocket chart next to the calendar. Move a fun "pointer" (such as a flag-topped pencil) under the words, and have students read the sentence aloud. Add sentences to the pocket chart on each special day.

GUESS WHAT I HAVE

Discuss the special days and give each student a photocopy of one of the special-day cards. (Two or three students may have the same card.) Have students take turns describing their cards without revealing the special days, such as *This is the day we celebrate the animals that sleep through winter.* Invite the student who guesses Hibernation Day to attach the card to the calendar.

TREAT BAGS

Place each special-day card and a small corresponding treat or prize in a resealable plastic bag. For example, place candy corn in a bag for Corn on the Cob Day. On the first day of the month, pin the bags on a bulletin board near the calendar. Remove the cards from the bags and attach them to the calendar as you discuss each day. When the special day arrives, remove the corresponding bag's contents and discuss them. Choose a student to keep the contents as a special reward.

LITERATURE MATCHUP

Have students sit in two lines facing each other. Provide each member of one group with a special-day card and each member of the other group with books whose subjects match the special-day cards held by the other group. Invite students to match cards and books, come forward in pairs, and introduce the day and book. Display the books near the calendar for students to read.

MINI-BOOKS

Reproduce numbered special-day cards so each student has a set. Have students sequence and staple their cards to make mini-books. Invite students to read their books and take them home to share with family members.

CREATIVE WRITING

Have each student glue a copy of a special-day card to a piece of construction paper. Invite students to illustrate and write about their special days. Have students share their writing. Display the writing near the calendar.

LUNCH SACK GAME

Provide each student with a paper lunch sack, a photocopy of each special-day card, and 15 index cards. Have students decorate the sacks for the month. Invite students to color the special-day cards and write on separate index cards a word or sentence describing each day. Have students place special-day cards and index cards in the sacks. Ask students to trade sacks, empty the contents, and match index cards to special-day cards.

SPECIAL-DAY BOX

One week before a special day, provide each student with a photocopied special-day card, an empty check box or shoe box, and a four-page blank book. Ask each student to take the box, book, and card home to prepare a special-day-box presentation. Have students write about their special day on the four book pages and place in the box small pictures or artifacts relating to the day. Ask students to decorate the boxes and glue their special-day cards to the top. Have students bring the completed boxes to school on the special day and give their presentations as an introduction to the day.

CHILDREN'S BOOK WEEK

Third Week in November

National Children's Book Week is the perfect time to share a favorite book with the class. Students will enjoy learning about their favorite authors as well as authoring books of their own.

LITERATURE LINKS

Amelia Bedelia by Peggy Parish

Arthur's Reading Race by Marc Brown

Aunt Isabel Tells a Good One by Kate Duke

How a Book Is Made by Aliki

I Can Read CTP Learn to Read Series

I Took My Frog to the Library by Eric A. Kimmel

Library Lil by Suzanne Williams

Read for Me, Mama by Vashanti Rahaman

Sorry, Miss Folio! by Jo Furtado

The Tale of Thomas Mead by Pat Hutchins

WE LOVE READING! BULLETIN BOARD

Ask students to design a book cover on construction paper for their favorite book and have them draw their head above the book to look as if they are reading it. Students can draw their hands on the sides of the book cover to look as if they are holding it. Have students cut out their drawing and use markers or paint to color it. Display the drawings on a bulletin board titled *We Love Reading!*

MATERIALS
▲ construction paper
▲ scissors
▲ markers or paint/ paintbrushes

BEAR BREAKFAST

MATERIALS
▲ family letter
▲ breakfast treats

Start off Children's Book Week with a BEAR (Be Enthusiastic About Reading!) Breakfast. Send home a note to families asking them to help their child select a favorite book to bring to school and share with their classmates. Solicit donations for mini-muffins, donut holes, or coffee cake along with milk or juice to serve for the BEAR breakfast. Have students sit in a circle with their favorite book. Invite students to share their favorite picture or read their favorite page. As each student shares a favorite story, invite the rest of the class to enjoy a breakfast snack. As an extension, have students share about favorite books in small groups or book clubs each week.

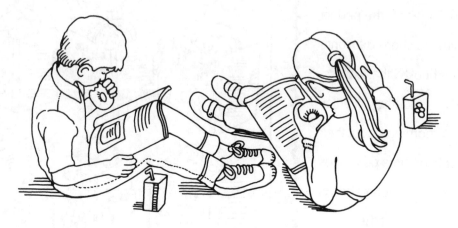

BOOK SACKS

MATERIALS
▲ construction paper
▲ crayons or markers
▲ scissors
▲ glue
▲ paper grocery sacks
▲ books

Have each student draw a bear on construction paper, cut out the bear, and glue the bear to a paper grocery sack. Have students write on the sack *I am a BEARy good reader!* and fill the sack with 1–3 books from the classroom library that they are able to read. Throughout Children's Book Week, encourage students to take their book sacks to partner-read with classmates, read on the playground, or read to younger students. Students can take home their sack at the end of the week to read stories to their families.

MUSICAL BOOK SWAP

MATERIALS
▲ family letter
▲ books
▲ grocery sack
▲ music box

Arrange for your class to have a book swap. Send home a letter to families asking them to help their child select a book they have already read and would be willing to exchange for another book. Throughout Children's Book Week, collect these books in a grocery sack. (Be sure to have a few extra books available.) Have students sit in a large circle. Open a music box and, while the music plays, have students pass the sack filled with books. When the music stops, the student holding the sack gets to select a book from it to take home and read. That student then leaves the circle and can open and close the music box for the next round of the game. The game continues until everyone receives a new book.

GROW A "BOOKSTALK"

MATERIALS
▲ Leaf reproducible (page 14)
▲ crayons
▲ green butcher paper

Create a green butcher-paper stalk along a corner wall in your classroom. Have students record book titles and authors on the Leaf reproducible after they finish reading a book. Invite students to color the "leaf" and attach it to the stalk titled *(Teacher's name) and the Bookstalk.* Watch your "bookstalk" fill with leaves!

Miss Naples
and the
Bookstalk

ROYAL READER DAY

Invite a different guest to come to your classroom each Friday in November. Have students suggest nominees and send letters to the invited guests. Ask each guest to bring a favorite children's book to read aloud. Request that the guest RSVP to the class's invitation. At the arrival of the guest reader, have volunteers roll out a red carpet that leads to a gold-painted "throne." Have a welcoming committee greet the guest with a red velvet cape and jeweled crown. Play trumpet music on an audiocassette as the guest is led to the throne. Have students cheer for their royal readers. Be sure to have students write thank-you notes afterward.

BOOK FLOATS

Invite students to cover shoe boxes or cereal boxes with construction paper and create parade "floats" that describe their favorite books. Students can use art supplies, old magazines, and plastic or clay figures to decorate the floats. Line up the floats and invite another class to watch the parade!

LETTER TO THE AUTHOR

Invite students to write letters to their favorite authors. This is a good time to discuss the parts of a letter and how to address an envelope. Encourage students to include their first and last name, home or school address, age, favorite book titles and characters, the reason why the author is their favorite, and a self-addressed, stamped envelope.

Gail Gibbons
Goose Green
Corinth, VT 05039

BOOK TALKS

Invite students to pretend they are a character from a story they have read. They can even come to school dressed as the character. Invite students to give a "book talk," that is, a description of a book character's life and adventures from the character's point of view. To begin the book talks, have students complete "in character" sentences such as the following: *My name is _____. I live _____. My best friend is _____. The most important thing that happened to me is _____. I can't wait to _____.* Invite classmates to ask the "character" questions.

BOOK QUILT

HOME ACTIVITY

Ask each student to select a book to be remembered in a quilt. Send home a cloth square and permanent markers or puffy paints and ask students to decorate the square with something interesting from the book. Use a glue gun to bind the pieces together. Use the quilt to promote additional discussions of the books. Invite students to take turns taking the quilt home to share with their families.

Frederick

Frog & Toad Together

Ira Sleeps Over

Miss Rumphius

LEAF

I read _____
(title)

by _____
(author)

Name _____

TERRIFIC TURKEYS

Turkey is traditionally served at Thanksgiving in honor of the first Thanksgiving, which took place in 1621. Native Americans raised turkey for food as early as A.D. 1000. Students will gobble like turkeys over these "turkey-rific" activities!

LITERATURE LINKS

Gracias, the Thanksgiving Turkey
by Joy Cowley

It's Thanksgiving
by Jack Prelutsky

McGuire's Turkey
by Peaches Smith

One Tough Turkey
by Steven Kroll

A Turkey for Thanksgiving
by Eve Bunting

Turkey's Gift to the People
by Ani Rucki

Turkeys That Fly and Turkeys That Don't
by Allan Fowler

'Twas the Night Before Thanksgiving
by Dav Pilkey

GRATEFUL TURKEY BULLETIN BOARD

Discuss with students what they are thankful for and invite them to record it on a copy of the Pumpkin reproducible. Roll brown construction paper into a cylinder shape to make a turkey neck. Attach to the neck a brown construction-paper circle for a turkey head and attach to a bulletin board. Add a red wattle, yellow beak, yellow legs, and facial features. Attach men's old neckties to the base of the turkey neck to form a body with tail feathers. Title the bulletin board *Don't Be a Turkey. Count Your Blessings!* Have students add their pumpkins to the bulletin board.

MATERIALS
▲ Pumpkin reproducible (page 22)
▲ brown, red, and yellow construction paper
▲ men's old neckties
▲ scissors
▲ markers

TURKEY TREATS

Have students place a chocolate-striped shortbread cookie on waxed paper. Invite students to use frosting as "glue" to attach two almonds at the bottom of the cookie for turkey feet. Then have students spread frosting on the center of the cookie, press the end of another cookie into the frosting (so that the second cookie is standing on edge as "feathers"), and place a caramel candy in front of the second cookie to be the turkey's head. Have students add to the caramel head a candy-corn nose and red hots for eyes. Wrap the turkey treats in cellophane for students to take home to eat.

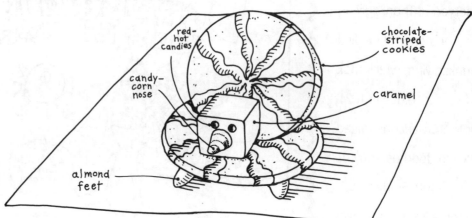

TURKEY CENTERPIECE

Have students trace on brown construction paper the turkey from the Turkey Centerpiece reproducible and cut it out. Have students trace their handprints from red, yellow, green, and orange construction paper, two from each color and cut them out. Help students overlap four handprints and staple them together to form the feathers of the turkey. Have students staple four more handprints together in the same manner and staple the second set of feathers so the fingers extend slightly higher than the first set. For a three-dimensional effect, curve the turkey and staple its sides to the "feathers" so the turkey's feet hang below the handprints. Place a glass or salt shaker in the center of the turkey to help it stand up on its own and curve the turkey's feet forward. Have students place their turkeys on the center of their Thanksgiving table.

TURKEY LURKEY

Have students accordion-fold a 4" (10 cm) brown construction-paper strip. Have them glue one end of the strip to the center of a small brown circle "head" and the other end to the center of a large brown circle "body." Have students glue two lima bean "eyes" to the small circle and use black marker to add pupils. Students can cut a construction-paper beak and wattle and glue them to the turkey face. Have students accordion-fold colorful construction-paper strips for feathers and glue them to the top back of the turkey body. Have students accordion-fold two long construction-paper strips for legs and glue them to the bottom of the circle. Invite students to cut out triangles at the end for feet. Display turkeys around the classroom for a festive display.

TEN LITTLE TURKEYS

Write a phrase from "Ten Little Turkey Children" on separate sheets of large brown construction paper to make a big book. Have each student paint the palm and thumb of one hand brown and the four fingers yellow, orange, green, and red. Have students each press their hand above the song text on the brown construction paper the appropriate number of times so that the number of "turkeys" match the text. Students can add legs to their turkeys and a red oval below the thumbprint. Have each student add an eye to the thumbprint. Bind the pages into a *Ten Little Turkey Children* class big book.

Ten Little Turkey Children
(to the tune of "Ten Little Indians")

One little, two little, three little turkeys,
Four little, five little, six little turkeys,
Seven little, eight little, nine little turkeys,
Ten little turkey children.

TURKEY GRAPH

Copy the Turkey reproducible onto a transparency, project the image onto the wall using an overhead, and trace the enlarged turkey on brown butcher paper. Draw different favorite Thanksgiving food items on small paper plates and glue the plates to the bottom of the turkey to create a graph. Have students draw their favorite Thanksgiving foods on paper squares and place them above the paper plates on the turkey graph. Discuss which foods were the favorites.

MATERIALS
- ▲ Turkey reproducible (page 24)
- ▲ transparency
- ▲ overhead projector
- ▲ brown butcher paper
- ▲ small paper plates
- ▲ glue
- ▲ crayons or markers
- ▲ 4" (10 cm) paper squares

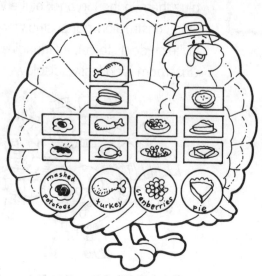

TURKEY TROT

MATERIALS
- ▲ round red balloons
- ▲ oblong yellow balloons
- ▲ rubber bands
- ▲ scissors
- ▲ tagboard
- ▲ masking tape
- ▲ paint/paintbrushes or markers

Invite students to blow up a red balloon and knot the end to make a turkey body. Have students blow up a yellow balloon about halfway to make a turkey head (so there is an uninflated "nose" at one end) and then knot the balloon. Invite students to tie an uninflated red balloon to the nose to make the turkey's wattle. Students can attach the knotted-off ends of the body and head together by wrapping a rubber band around them. Have students cut feet from tagboard and attach them to the bottom of the turkey with masking tape. Invite students to use paint or markers to draw a face and feathers on their balloon turkey. Invite students to hold a race to see who can bop their turkey across the room first. Teach students the song "The Turkey" and have them sing it in a round.

The Turkey

(to the tune of "Row, Row, Row Your Boat")
The turkey is a funny bird.
His head goes wobble, wobble.
And all he says is just one word:
Gobble, gobble, gobble.

FIVE FAT TURKEYS FINGERPLAY

Have each student color and cut out five turkeys from the Turkey Finger Puppets reproducible. Have students glue the end flaps together to fit their fingers. Invite students to say the poem "Five Fat Turkeys" while wearing their finger puppets.

Five Fat Turkeys	Motions
Five fat turkeys on Thanksgiving Day,	
Said, "Gobble, gobble, gobble, let's run away."	
The first one said, "I don't want to be dinner."	(Raise first finger.)
The second one said, "I wish I were thinner."	(Raise second finger.)
The third one said, "It's getting late."	(Raise third finger.)
The fourth one said, "Let's hurry past the gate."	(Raise fourth finger.)
The fifth one said, "Here comes the cook."	(Raise fifth finger.)
Then five fat turkeys stopped to have a look.	
The cook was fast and grabbed them all.	(Hide hand behind back.)
He served them in the dining hall.	
But that Thanksgiving Day turned out the best,	
For each fat turkey was a guest!	(Show open hand.)

THE WISHBONE

Read aloud the poem "The Wishbone" from *It's Thanksgiving*. Invite students to make a wish and write on the Wishbone reproducible why they would like this wish to come true. Challenge students to think of nonmaterial wishes, such as wishing for the health of a family member.

TURKEY HATS

Have students trace on folded brown construction paper, and cut out, the Feather reproducible. Have students trace on folded red construction paper, and cut out, the Turkey Hat reproducible. Have students glue colorful construction-paper squares on the feather pattern. Help students staple the turkey head to the feather pattern so it fits each student's head. Invite students to act out "Three Turkey Gobblers" while wearing their turkey hats.

Three Turkey Gobblers

The night before Thanksgiving,
When I had gone to bed,
I heard three turkey gobblers,
And this is what they said.

The first turkey said,
"I think that I will go,
And hide behind the haystack,
Where no one will know."

The second turkey said,
"I think I'll find a tree,
And hide up in the branches,
Where no one will see."

The third turkey said,
"I think it would be fun,
To hide the farmer's hatchet,
Then, run, run, run."

On Thanksgiving morning,
When the farmer came around,
Those three turkey gobblers,
Could not be found.

TURKEY TIME

MATERIALS

▲ paper lunch sacks
▲ newspaper
▲ wiggly eyes
▲ red balloons
▲ paper grocery sacks
▲ large rubber bands
▲ art supplies (crayons or markers, paint/paintbrushes, glue)

Have each student stuff the bottom of a paper lunch sack with crumpled newspaper to form a turkey head and twist the top of the sack to form a long, skinny neck. Have students glue wiggly eyes and a red balloon wattle onto the "face." For the turkey's body, each student snips through the front of a large grocery sack to make a hole an inch (2.5 cm) from the bottom and fits the neck into it. Students stuff the body two-thirds full with newspaper and close the top of the sack with a rubber band. To make tail feathers, each student cuts four large half-circles from separate grocery sacks, decorates them with art supplies, and glues them in layers to the body.

deflated balloon

OUR FAMILIES LOVE TURKEY

MATERIALS

▲ Turkey Centerpiece reproducible (page 23)
▲ transparency
▲ overhead projector
▲ large construction-paper feathers
▲ brown butcher paper

HOME ACTIVITY

Copy the Turkey Centerpiece reproducible onto a transparency, project the image onto the wall using an overhead, and trace it on brown butcher paper. Send home with each student a large construction-paper turkey feather. Have students work with their families to decorate the feather with a pattern or collage of items, such as pictures of food they love to eat or pictures of activities they like to do. Invite students to share how they chose to decorate their feather. Display feathers on a wall or bulletin board. Attach the turkey slightly below the feathers for an attractive display.

PUMPKIN

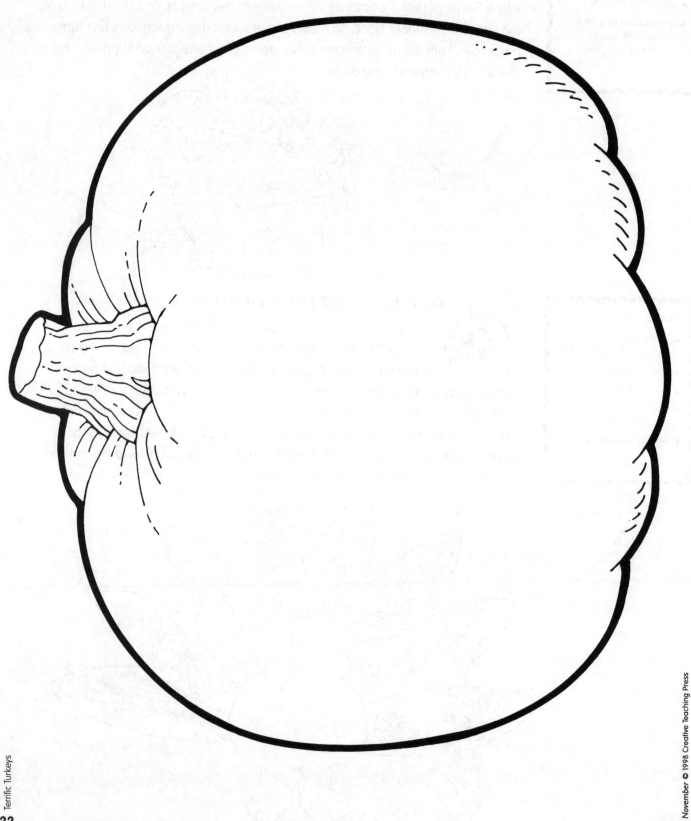

TURKEY CENTERPIECE

TURKEY

TURKEY FINGER PUPPETS

WISHBONE

I wish for _____

_____

_____

_____

_____

_____

_____

FEATHER

Place on fold.

TURKEY HAT

Place on fold.

November © 1998 Creative Teaching Press

FAMILY WEEK

Families can provide love, mutual caring, and understanding. This week was designated by Presidential Proclamation as a time to salute the contributions of the American family.

LITERATURE LINKS

Adoption Is for Always
by Linda W. Girard

All Kinds of Families
by Norma Simon

Amelia Bedelia's Family Album
by Peggy Parish

Butterfly Boy by Gerardo Suzan

Celebrating Families
by Rosmarie Hausherr

A Chair for My Mother
by Vera B. Williams

*Henry and Mudge
in the Family Trees*
by Cynthia Rylant

The Important Book
by Margaret Wise Brown

Long Ago and Today
CTP Learn to Read Series

Love You Forever
by Robert Munsch

THE FACES OF OUR FAMILIES BULLETIN BOARD

Invite students to bring in photographs or draw pictures of themselves with their family members. Collect the pictures and mount them on a construction-paper border. Cover the students' faces with sticky notes and number each family picture. Attach the pictures to a bulletin board titled *The Faces of Our Families.* Invite students to guess which student belongs with which family. Once families are identified, invite each student to share something about his or her family.

MATERIALS
▲ family photographs or drawings
▲ construction paper
▲ sticky notes

MATERIALS

▲ 6" (15 cm) white construction-paper squares
▲ crayons
▲ chart paper
▲ glue
▲ writing paper

FAMILY GRAPH

Have each student fold and cut the top two corners of a construction-paper square to make a house shape with a pointed roof. Ask students to draw the people in their families on the house. Have students write the number of family members on the roof. Invite students to attach their houses to a bar graph to indicate family size. Later, have students glue their house to writing paper and write or dictate something about each family member.

MATERIALS

▲ November Newsletter (page 95)

FAMILY NEWSLETTER

HOME ACTIVITY

Send home with students a copy of the November Newsletter and invite students and their family members to record on it memorable times together. Families can write about special events or memories, such as vacations, birthdays, and favorite moments. Invite students to include drawings or photographs of themselves with their family members. Invite students to share their family newsletters with the class.

FAMILY TIME TOGETHER

Have students draw, color, and cut out pictures of each of their family members and write on a sentence strip a sentence describing one thing their family likes to do together. As a class, decorate a large piece of butcher paper with pictures of houses and glue each student's family pictures in front of a house, attaching the sentence strip below the picture. Title the butcher paper *Family Fun Time,* and display it on a bulletin board or wall.

THE MOST IMPORTANT THING

Read aloud *The Important Book.* Model for students how to write about their own families using the sentence pattern from the book. Have each student write or dictate a poem about his or her family. For example:

The most important thing about my family is that they love me!

My family _____.

My family _____.

My family _____.

But, the most important thing about my family is that they love me!

Ask families to send in pictures of family members for students to cut out and glue to their poems as decoration, or have students illustrate their poems.

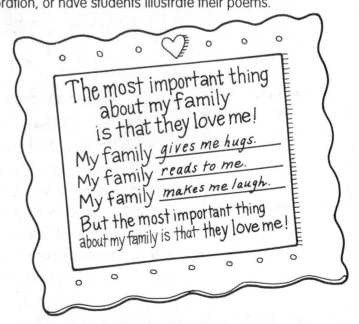

MATERIALS

▲ family photographs
▲ blank journals
▲ glue
▲ crayons or markers

FAMILY TIME BOOKS

Ask each student to bring in a family photograph and glue it to the cover of a blank journal titled *Family Time.* Have students copy on each page the frame *My (family member) likes to _____.* For example, *My sister likes to bake cookies.* Have students write on the last page *But together we like to _____.* Invite students to complete the frames and illustrate each page. Students can read their books aloud to classmates.

MATERIALS

▲ *Long Ago and Today* CTP Learn to Read Series
▲ construction paper
▲ crayons or markers

LONG AGO AND TODAY

Read aloud and discuss *Long Ago and Today.* Ask students what their parents or grandparents did long ago that was different from what they themselves do today. Invite students to divide construction paper in half lengthwise and write on one side *Long ago, my (relative) _____.* Have them write on the other side *Today, I _____.* Have students illustrate their papers.

MATERIALS

▲ family letter

NO TV DAY

HOME ACTIVITY

Tell students one way they can celebrate family week is by not watching television. Send home a letter asking families to turn off the TV for 24 hours and spend the time doing other activities, such as reading, drawing, playing games, going to the park, or taking a nature walk around the neighborhood. Challenge families to try keeping the television off for an entire week. Students may discover new interests and ways to communicate with their families. Invite students to share how they spent the time they would normally have spent watching TV.

FABULOUS FALL FEASTS

Fall brings a harvest of foods fit for a feast. Celebrate the plentiful harvest with these scrumptious activities.

HARVEST BULLETIN BOARD

Give students one paper grocery sack each, and have them roll down the top of the sack. Cut wide strips from extra grocery sacks. Have students twist the strips and staple them to the sides of their sack to form handles. Explain to students that the sack will be their harvest basket. Invite students to draw on construction paper fall harvested foods, such as pumpkins, corn, squash, nuts, acorns, cranberries, or dates to go in their basket. Have students paint front and back sides of each food, let them dry, and staple the two sides together, leaving an opening to stuff with crumpled newspaper. Then have students staple the openings closed. Invite students to put their "foods" in their harvest basket and write on their basket *Farmer (student's name) harvested (food names).* Attach the baskets to a bulletin board titled *Room ____ Farmers' Fall Harvest.*

MATERIALS
▲ paper grocery sacks
▲ construction paper
▲ paint/paintbrushes
▲ stapler
▲ newspaper

FALL FRUIT

MATERIALS
- ▲ orange, purple, yellow, red, green, and black construction paper
- ▲ scissors
- ▲ chalk pastels
- ▲ cotton balls
- ▲ glue

Have each student cut out from construction paper a yellow pear, red apple, green and purple grapes, and an orange pumpkin. Invite students to gently rub along the left side and bottom of each fruit with chalk pastels the same color as the fruit. Then have students blend brown chalk with the other chalk. Students can use light-green chalk on the pear. Invite students to use cotton balls to soften the line edges. Have students glue their fall fruit display to black construction paper, and display the fall harvest around the room.

CORNUCOPIA

MATERIALS
- ▲ Cornucopia reproducible (page 38)
- ▲ tape
- ▲ tagboard
- ▲ plastic wrap
- ▲ permanent markers
- ▲ aluminum foil

Have students tape a copy of the Cornucopia reproducible to a piece of tagboard. Help students cover the reproducible with plastic wrap and tape it in place. Invite students to color in the cornucopia shape on the plastic wrap with permanent markers before they outline the shape with a black permanent marker. Have students lightly crumple a sheet of aluminum foil and then smooth it out over a piece of tagboard. Help students remove their plastic-wrap artwork, place it on the foil-covered side of the tagboard, and tape it to the back side.

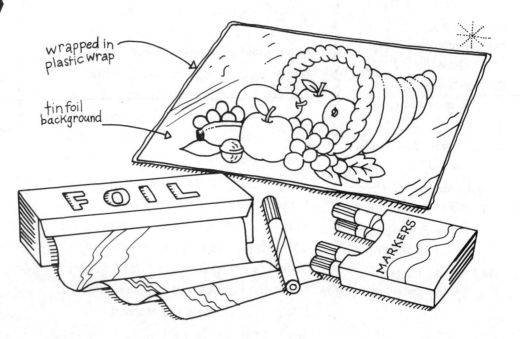

wrapped in plastic wrap

tin foil background

APPLE PIE BOOK

MATERIALS

▲ scalloped scissors
▲ paper plates
▲ tan, dark-brown, and white construction paper
▲ scissors
▲ glue
▲ crayons
▲ cotton balls

Using scalloped scissors, cut tan construction-paper "crust" circles to cover paper plates. Cut smaller dark-brown construction-paper circles for the bottom crust and have students glue them to the inside of their paper plate. Poke a hole in the center of the tan circle. Have students cut two diagonal lines from the center across the circle within an inch (2.5 cm) of the other side, creating four "pie pieces." Help students staple the tan circle to the rim of the paper plate. Invite students to fold back each pie piece. Have students choose how many of three different apples they want to add to their apple pie and write that on the underside of three pie pieces. Have students add the total number of apples used and record that number on the underside of the last pie piece. For example, *I added 5 red apples. I added 9 green apples. I added 6 yellow apples. Twenty apples make a yummy apple pie!* Invite students to draw the different-colored apples on construction paper, cut them out, and glue them to the dark-brown "crust" so that when each flap is lifted, the correct number of apples appears in the pie. Have students stretch cotton balls as "whipped cream" to decorate the top of their pie. Students can draw designs on the top of the pie crust to resemble a real pie.

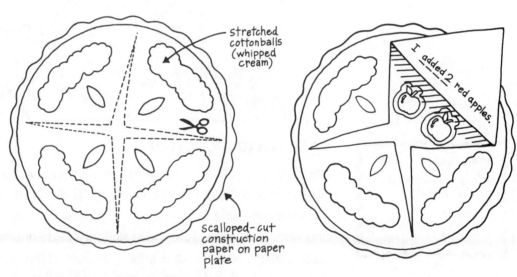

stretched cottonballs (whipped cream)

I added 2 red apples.

scalloped-cut construction paper on paper plate

HARVEST VOCABULARY

MATERIALS

▲ harvest foods (corn, squash, pumpkins)
▲ manipulatives (craft sticks, milk caps, white beans, wooden cubes)
▲ marker

Bring to class some foods that have been recently harvested in your area, such as corn, squash, or pumpkins. Print letters from harvest food names on an assortment of manipulatives such as craft sticks, milk caps, dry white beans, or wooden cubes. Place the manipulatives on the table with harvest foods. Invite students to use the manipulatives to spell words.

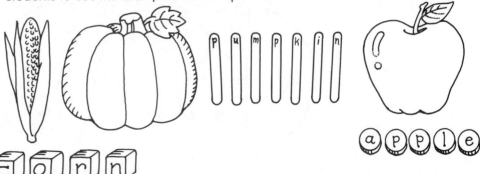

TIP-TOP TABLE MANNERS PARTY

Ask students to dress up for a fancy fall feast. Give each student a large and small plate, knife, spoon, cup, napkin, and two forks to correctly place on a desk or table. Explain that forks belong on the left and the knife and soup spoon belong on the right. Remind students that they always begin eating with the flatware furthest from their plate. Tell students that their bread plate belongs on the left and their cup belongs on the right. Explain that the first thing they must do after they sit down at a table is open their napkin halfway and put it in their lap. Explain that a used napkin should not be placed on the table during a meal. When finished eating, students can place their napkin to the left of their plate. Demonstrate how to pass serving dishes to the right. Tell students they are not to begin eating until everyone is seated and the host or hostess lifts his or her fork. Enjoy a light meal together using tip-top table manners.

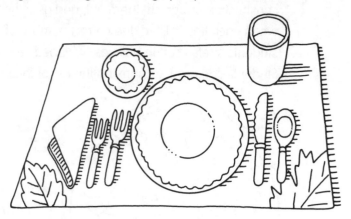

FALL FOOD FRACTIONS

Give each student four construction-paper circles. Ask students to pretend the circles are pies. Have students color one "pie" and write *one whole* on it. Have each student divide another pie in half. Invite students to color one half of the pie and write $\frac{1}{2}$ on each piece. Have students divide another pie into four equal pieces, color one piece, and write $\frac{1}{4}$ on each of the four pieces. Have students divide another pie into eight equal pieces, color one piece, and write $\frac{1}{8}$ on each piece. Have students cut all the pie pieces apart. Ask students how many eighths equal one half. Have students cover the half piece with eighths to find the answer. Ask them other fraction questions, such as *How many eighths equal one fourth?* or *How many fourths equal one whole?* Have students hold up different fractions of the pie to practice identifying fractions.

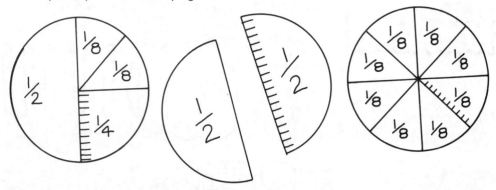

HARVEST STEW

Send home a letter asking families to send in a washed and chopped vegetable to add to a harvest stew. Add a turkey leg and chicken or beef broth to a slow cooker. Invite each student to pour his or her vegetable into a measuring cup before adding it to the pot. Then record on chart paper what each student added. For example, *Mrs. Johnson added 1 turkey leg and 2 cans of broth. Joellyn added $\frac{1}{2}$ cup of onions.* While the soup cooks, invite each student to write and illustrate on construction paper what he or she added to the stew. Bind the pages together for a class book titled *Harvest Stew.* When the stew is cooked, debone the meat and serve.

Carolea added $\frac{1}{2}$ cup of carrots to our Harvest Stew.

HARVEST STEW
by Mrs. Oertle's Class

FAVORITE FAMILY FALL FOODS

HOME ACTIVITY

Send home a note asking families to prepare together a favorite fall food, such as caramel apples, sweet potatoes, or pumpkin bread. Invite students to bring to class samples of the food they prepared. Ask students to describe their family's favorite fall food and share samples of the food.

Our Favorite Family Fall Foods

cornbread   yams   pumpkin pie   cranberries   mashed potatoes   Mama's surprise

CORNUCOPIA

SANDWICH DAY

November 3

John Montague, the fourth Earl of Sandwich, created the world's first fast food on this date when he invented the sandwich so he wouldn't have to take time out of his busy day to eat. Celebrate Sandwich Day with these mouth-watering activities.

The Sandwich Shuffle

Touch your toes for turkey.
Leap for lettuce.
Cheer for cheese.
Twist for tomato.

CLAP CLAP

LITERATURE LINKS

1000 Silly Sandwiches
by Alan Benjamin

Bread and Jam for Frances
by Russell Hoban

Bread, Bread, Bread
by Ann Morris

Cat and Dog Make the Best, Biggest, Most Wonderful Cheese Sandwich
CTP Learn to Read Series

The Giant Jam Sandwich
by John Vernon Lord

Sam's Sandwich
by David Pelham

So Hungry! by Harriet Ziefert

THE SANDWICH SHUFFLE

Brainstorm sandwich ingredients with your students and list them on chart paper. Assign each ingredient an action that has the same beginning letter as the ingredient, such as bow for bread, jump for jam, leap for lettuce, twist for tomato, march for mustard, pop up for pickles, wiggle for white bread, and do a jumping jack for jack cheese. Have students move to a large, open space and invite them to do the motions as they read the ingredients. Then, have students do the motions without saying the words. Encourage students to create their own sandwich shuffles using other ingredients from the list.

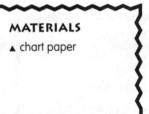

MATERIALS
▲ chart paper

Sandwich Day

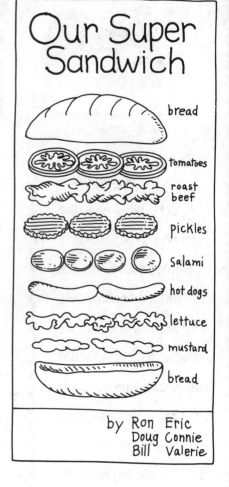

OUR SUPER-SIZE SANDWICHES

In advance, send home a note asking family members to send in two sandwich items with their child to celebrate Sandwich Day. Divide your class into small groups. Give each group a French bread loaf and a plastic knife. Have each group combine what they brought to school to create one giant sandwich to share. Have each team illustrate their sandwich on construction paper, label each ingredient, and create a name for their sandwich. Have teams share their drawings. Cut the sandwiches into small slices. Invite students to try a few sandwiches. Display posters in the room. Teach students the "Super Sandwich" song.

Super Sandwich

(to the tune of: "Itsy Bitsy Spider")

My super lunch sandwich is really fun to eat,
Pickles, tomatoes, cheese and deli meat.
When I get too full and can't eat another bite,
I put it in my lunch box and eat it at night.

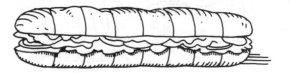

PITA POCKETS

Invite students to choose three different deli items and put them inside a pita pocket. Then, have students fold construction paper in half and cut the corners to create a paper pita pocket. Have students cut out paper ingredients to match the ingredients in their real pita pockets. Have students write the frame *(Student's name) put (ingredient), (ingredient), and (ingredient) in his/her pita pocket.* Then invite students to eat their real pitas. Have students take their paper pita pockets home to share with their families.

MATERIALS

▲ pita pockets cut in half

▲ deli items

▲ condiments

▲ plastic knives

▲ napkins or paper plates

▲ construction paper

▲ scissors

Ernie put bologna, lettuce, and tomato in his pita pocket.

ELECTION DAY

It is important for citizens to exercise their right to vote at all levels of government. Teach students more about the voting process so they can share in the excitement of Election Day.

LITERATURE LINKS

Arthur Meets the President
by Marc Brown

The Berenstain Bears and the Big Election
by Stan and Jan Berenstain

I Speak for the Women: A Story About Lucy Stone
by Stephanie McPherson

The Mayor: Signs of Protest
by Pat Lakin, et al.

Our Elections by Richard Steins

The Voice of the People
by Betsy Maestro

The Vote: Making Your Voice Heard
by Linda Scher

Voting and Elections
by Dennis B. Fradin

WHO'S IN CHARGE?

On separate sheets of construction paper, write *Mayor, Governor,* and *President.* Invite three volunteers to hold up the signs and three volunteers to hold up city, state, and country maps. Ask the volunteers to pair up (mayor with the city map, governor with the state map, and president with the country map). Ask classmates to call out *Mayor, city; Governor, state; and President, country.* Invite the volunteers to give their sign or map to different students, and have them repeat the activity in the front of the class.

MATERIALS
▲ construction paper
▲ city map
▲ state map
▲ country map

EVERY VOTE COUNTS

To hold a class election, create a class ballot showing presidential candidates, an issue students understand, or a choice of three favorite books. Set up a large box where students can cast secret ballots. Explain the concept "majority rules." Assign students to tally votes and announce election results. Count the years before they can vote in public elections.

MAJORITY RULES

Have students record some of their favorites, such as favorite ice-cream flavor, book, toy, food, pet, song, color, school subject, or thing to do. Tally the favorite choices in each category. Record the top two choices in each category and invite students to vote for their favorites from the choices given. Write the elected favorites in a class booklet titled *Majority Rules.*

SHOOT THE HOOPS DAY

The first basketball was a soccer ball and the hoops were peach baskets. James Naismith (whose birthday is today) invented the game of basketball in 1891 so he could play an active indoor game in winter. Students will be ahead of the game with these all-star activities.

LITERATURE LINKS

Allie's Basketball Dream
by Barbara E. Barber

Basketball
by Bert Rosenthal

Basketball ABC:
The NBA Alphabet
by Florence C. Mayers

Basketball's High Flyers
by Nathan Aaseng

Hoops
by Robert Burleigh

Swish!
by Bill Martin, Jr.

SLAM DUNK BULLETIN BOARD

Cut out the center of a large plastic lid and use the rim to create a basketball hoop. Tie yarn around the sides for the net and attach the basketball hoop to a bulletin board titled *This Work Is a Slam Dunk!* Invite students to color and cut out a basketball from the Basketballs reproducible. Have students glue a photograph of themselves in the center of the ball. Invite students to choose their favorite work from the week to display on the bulletin board. Attach the basketballs with student photographs to the corner of their favorite work.

MATERIALS

▲ scissors
▲ large plastic lid (from a coffee can or popcorn canister)
▲ yarn
▲ Basketballs reproducible (page 45)
▲ crayons or markers
▲ glue
▲ student photographs

BASKETBALL CAMP

Arrange for older students to work with your class and coach your students on basketball skills. Give the "coaches" whistles to wear and have your students call each of them *Coach.* Set up stations for students to practice dribbling (dribble around chairs), passing (chest pass, bounce pass, and overhead pass), and shooting baskets (shoot into trash cans, then hoops). End the activity with refreshments for everyone and a question-answer period. Have students write thank-you notes to their coaches.

MATERIALS

▲ whistles
▲ chairs
▲ trash cans
▲ basketball hoops
▲ basketballs
▲ refreshments
▲ stationery

SHOOT AND SCORE

Make a list of problems students should be able to answer, such as simple math equations or spelling words. Use masking tape to delineate a "free-throw line" on the classroom floor. Divide the class into two teams and have each team line up behind the free-throw line. Ask a question to the student in front from one team. Have the student try to throw a crumpled paper ball into the trash can and then answer the question. If the student answered the question correctly, he or she can take another shot and earn a point. Otherwise, the student goes to the end of the line and a student from the other team gets a turn.

MATERIALS

▲ list of questions
▲ masking tape
▲ crumpled paper ball
▲ trash can

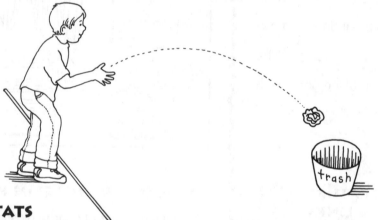

MATH STATS

Bring in the newspaper's sports section. Use basketball statistics to do mental math with your students. Ask students to find the difference between the final scores or the points individual players scored. Have students use mental math to add final game scores. (Ask younger students to count by tens until they reach the score or count backward beginning with a basketball score.) You can invite students to use tally marks on the chalkboard to record game scores.

MATERIALS

▲ newspaper (sports section)

BASKETBALLS

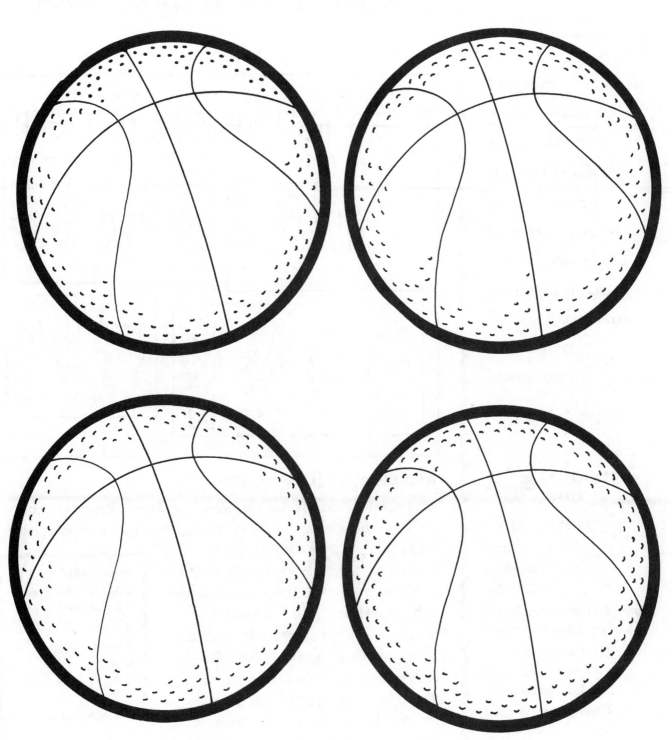

RED LEAF, YELLOW LEAF DAY

November 9

Lois Ehlert is a favorite children's author. She prefers cutting and pasting to drawing so her books are full of brightly colored collage. Celebrate her birthday on Red Leaf, Yellow Leaf Day with these colorful activities.

LITERATURE LINKS

Books by Lois Ehlert

Circus

Color Farm

Color Zoo

Eating the Alphabet: Fruits and Vegetables from A to Z

Feathers for Lunch

*Fish Eyes:
A Book You Can Count On*

Growing Vegetable Soup

Hands

Planting a Rainbow

Red Leaf, Yellow Leaf

Snowballs

Under My Nose

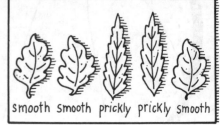

Can You See the Pattern?

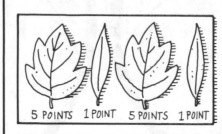

5 POINTS   1 POINT   5 POINTS   1 POINT

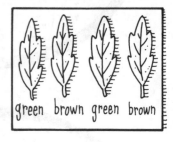

smooth   smooth   prickly   prickly   smooth

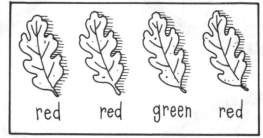

red   red   green   red

green   brown   green   brown

RED LEAF, YELLOW LEAF

Read aloud and discuss *Red Leaf, Yellow Leaf.* Take a class nature walk and invite each student to collect four leaves. Divide the class into groups of four. Invite students in each group to compile their leaves. Have groups sort their leaves into several categories such as leaves with several points, green leaves, colored leaves, round leaves, leaves with one point, smooth leaves, and prickly leaves. Then invite each group to create a pattern with their leaves, such as green leaf, green leaf, red leaf. Have each group glue their pattern to a sentence strip and label it. Display the leaf patterns on a bulletin board titled *Can You See the Pattern?*

MATERIALS

▲ *Red Leaf, Yellow Leaf* by Lois Ehlert
▲ leaves
▲ sentence strips
▲ glue
▲ crayons or markers

COLOR FARM SCENES

MATERIALS

▲ *Color Farm*
  by Lois Ehlert
▲ pattern blocks
▲ white construction
  paper
▲ crayons or markers

Read aloud and discuss *Color Farm.* Invite students to create their own colorful farm scenes. Have them trace pattern blocks onto construction paper to make object designs such as barns, tractors, fences, and farm animals. Then have students color their designs and label each item. Display the scenes on a bulletin board titled *Other Color Farms.*

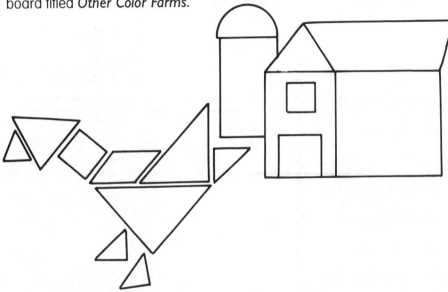

"EATING THE ALPHABET" TALLY

MATERIALS

▲ *Eating the Alphabet*
  by Lois Ehlert
▲ writing paper
▲ chart paper

Read aloud and discuss *Eating the Alphabet.* Have each student make a T-chart. Have students write *Have Tried* on the left side of the chart and *Have Not Tried* on the right side. Go through the book a second time and ask students to make a tally mark on the T-chart to show if they have or have not eaten the described food. Have students count their marks on each side of the chart and share their numbers. Show the students' "scores" on a class T-chart and invite the class to count by fives to find the numbers on both sides of the chart.

VETERANS DAY

My American Hero
by Charis

My hero is my mom. She loves me and works hard to take care of me. She's the best.

November 11

Veterans Day is dedicated to world peace and to the memory of all American veterans. In 1919 after the Treaty of Versailles ended World War I, President Wilson declared November 11 Armistice Day. Congress later changed the name to Veterans Day to honor all the men and women who have served in the armed forces.

LITERATURE LINKS

All Those Secrets of the World
by Jane Yolen

Buffalo Soldiers: The Story of Emanuel Stance
by Michael Bryant

The Wall
by Eve Bunting

War Boy: A Country Childhood
by Michael Forman

OUR HEROES

Discuss the word *hero* and the characteristics that heroes and heroines possess. Explain to the class that men and women who have fought for our country are often considered heroes. Ask students to think of someone they consider their hero. Encourage students to write on the Hero reproducible what makes that person a hero. Have students cut out their work and color it. Invite students to give or send their notes to their hero.

MATERIALS
▲ Hero reproducible (page 50)
▲ scissors
▲ crayons or markers

VETERAN FRIENDS

MATERIALS
▲ patriotic song lyrics

Ask students if they know anyone who has served in the armed forces—Army, Navy, Air Force, Marines, or Coast Guard. Contact the local VFW (Veterans of Foreign Wars) to invite local veterans to share their experiences with the class. Sing patriotic songs such as "America, the Beautiful," "You're a Grand Old Flag," or "My Country 'Tis of Thee." Be sure to have students write thank-you notes to the veterans who visit.

TIE A YELLOW RIBBON

MATERIALS
▲ yellow ribbon
▲ paint/paintbrushes
▲ star-shaped sponges
▲ cotton swabs
▲ construction paper
▲ scissors
▲ stapler

Explain to students that yellow ribbons tied outside homes and businesses show that servicemen and servicewomen on active duty are not forgotten. Invite students to tie yellow ribbons into bows and attach them as a border around a bulletin board titled *Honor Our Veterans*. Have students paint a flag on the center of the bulletin board using star-shaped sponges to make the stars. Tell students that the poppy has been a symbol of remembrance since World War I and was inspired by a poem about a French military cemetery. Invite students to dip their thumbs in red paint and press them on construction paper in the shape of a poppy. Have students add stems with thin paintbrushes. When the paint dries, have students dab the center of their poppies with a cotton swab dipped in black paint. Invite students to cut out their poppies and attach them to the bulletin board around the flag.

HERO

My American Hero

by _____

November © 1998 Creative Teaching Press

THANKSGIVING

Fourth Thursday in November

The Pilgrims arrived in Plymouth, Massachusetts, in 1620. After their first bountiful harvest, the Pilgrims prepared a feast to give thanks to God. They invited their Native American friends to join them. Thanksgiving has been celebrated since that day as a time to gather with family and friends and give thanks.

LITERATURE LINKS

Arthur's Thanksgiving
by Marc Brown

The First Thanksgiving
by Jean Craighead George

The First Thanksgiving
by Linda Hayward

If You Sailed on the Mayflower in 1620
by Ann McGovern

Molly's Pilgrim
by Barbara Cohen

Thanksgiving Day
by Gail Gibbons

The Thanksgiving Story
by Alice Dalgliesh

MAYFLOWER BULLETIN BOARD

Have students draw a face on the back side of a paper plate. Have students color and cut out either the boy or girl hat from the Pilgrim Boy and Girl reproducible. Have students glue the hats to the top of the plates. Make a large boat from brown butcher paper, write *Mayflower* on it, and attach it to a bulletin board. Cut out a large butcher-paper sail and mast. Sponge-paint white on blue construction-paper strips to form waves. Scatter the paper-plate Pilgrim faces on the boat. Title the bulletin board *Set Sail with Room _____*.

MATERIALS

▲ small paper plates
▲ crayons or markers
▲ Pilgrim Boy and Girl reproducible (page 59)
▲ scissors
▲ glue
▲ brown and white butcher paper
▲ sponge
▲ white paint
▲ blue construction-paper strips

NOW I AM FULL

MATERIALS
▲ paint/paintbrushes
▲ construction paper
▲ scissors
▲ glue
▲ yarn or raffia
▲ bookbinding materials

Have students brainstorm their favorite Thanksgiving foods and paint them on construction paper. When the pictures dry, have students cut out the foods and glue each item to a separate sheet of construction paper above the frame *In went the* _____. Invite students to paint a full-looking face on the last page over the sentence *Now I am full!* Invite students to add yarn or raffia hair to their picture. Bind each student's Thanksgiving book and invite students to title them *In Went . . . .*

In went the pumpkin pie.

Now I am full!

last page

PILGRIM BOY HATS

MATERIALS
▲ Pilgrim Hat reproducible (page 60)
▲ white crayons
▲ black and white construction paper
▲ scissors
▲ glue
▲ stapler

Have boy students use a white crayon to trace on folded black construction paper the Pilgrim Hat reproducible and have them cut it out. Have boys trace the buckles on white paper, cut them out, and glue them to the center of their hat. Help students staple black construction-paper strips to the sides of their hat. Staple the ends together to fit each student's head. Have students wear their hats and pilgrim outfits (page 54) for a Thanksgiving parade.

PILGRIM GIRL HATS

MATERIALS
▲ 9" x 12" (23 cm x 30.5 cm) white construction paper
▲ hole punch
▲ yarn

Invite the girls to fold up the long side of white construction paper 2" (5 cm). Then, have them hole-punch the bottom corner of each folded side and tie yarn to each hole. Invite girls to put the hat on with the fold side outward and tie a bow under their chin.

THANKSGIVING HAT CARDS

Have students cut out the Thanksgiving Card reproducible and fold on the fold line so the smaller portion becomes the front of the card. Ask students to write *Happy Thanksgiving* on the rim of the hat and write a message on the inside of the card. Invite students to add the band and buckle to the front of the card. Invite students to give their card to a family member or deliver it to a hospital or retirement home.

DOUBLE THE RECIPE

Invite students to use their math skills to increase recipe quantities to provide enough food for all students in the class to eat. Ask students how many apples they will need to make applesauce for the class if two apples serve one person. Have them solve other recipe conversions, such as how many pounds of butter they will need for four turkeys if they need one pound for one turkey or how many cups of sugar they will need to make five apple pies if two cups are needed for one pie. Invite students to record and illustrate the problems in their math journals and create some problems of their own.

MAYFLOWER VOYAGE

MATERIALS
▲ world map or globe
▲ paper
▲ The Pilgrim Story (pages 56–58)

Use a world map or globe to trace the voyage of the *Mayflower* from England to Holland to Cape Cod to Plymouth. Invite students to pretend they are on the voyage and send postcards from each place telling their friends or family about the voyage. Then, invite students to act out "The Pilgrim Story." Read the play aloud for younger students and have them create appropriate actions.

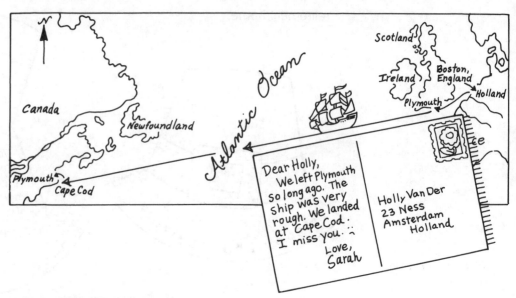

THANKSGIVING FEAST

MATERIALS
▲ Pilgrim reproducible (page 62)
▲ white and yellow construction paper
▲ black construction-paper strips
▲ 9" x 4" (23 cm x 10 cm) white construction paper
▲ scissors
▲ stapler
▲ glue
▲ gold brads
▲ food

Invite students to place the collar from the Pilgrim reproducible on folded white construction paper and cut it out. Have students make a cut on the back side from the center to the neckline so they can put on the collar. Give each student two black construction-paper strips that are stapled together at one end to make a belt. Have students put it around their waist and staple it to fit. Invite students to place the buckle pattern on yellow construction paper, cut it out, and glue it to the center of their belt. Give students two white construction-paper rectangles each. Have them wrap one around each wrist and secure it with a gold brad to make cuffs. Invite girls to wear cotton squares as aprons, and have all students wear their Pilgrim hats (page 52). Invite students to bring a favorite dish from home to create an in-class Thanksgiving meal.

GOOD NEWS

Ask students to search through newspapers and magazines to find only stories that could be considered good news. Have them underline or highlight a sentence or two from each story that summarizes the good news. Invite students to share some of the good news they are thankful for.

MATERIALS
▲ newspapers
▲ magazines

THANKFUL SURVEY

MATERIALS
▲ writing paper
▲ chart paper
▲ sentence strips

Invite students to survey family members, fellow students, teachers, or neighbors to find out what they are thankful for. When students return their surveys, have them categorize what people were thankful for according to the similarities, such as possessions, family, health, or experiences. Discuss and graph their findings according to main categories. Write observations on sentence strips around the graph.

More people were thankful for their friends than health.

More people were thankful for things they own than for things in nature.

What we're thankful for

45 40 35 30 25 20 15 10

family   health   possessions   experiences   nature   friends

PILGRIM DOLLS

MATERIALS
▲ *Molly's Pilgrim* by Barbara Cohen
▲ clothespins
▲ fabric scraps

HOME ACTIVITY

Read aloud and discuss *Molly's Pilgrim.* Explain that it is a true story about the author's family. Ask students to talk to their parents about where their ancestors came from. Invite students to make their own dolls dressed like the Pilgrims or in the traditional dress of their country's origin. Have students make their dolls using clothespins and fabric scraps, as in the story.

THE PILGRIM STORY

Act I
The Atlantic Ocean, on the *Mayflower*
October 1620

Characters
5 Pilgrim Children
3 Narrators

Child 1:   I'm tired of this ship. There's nothing to do and nowhere to go. And whenever there's a storm, I get seasick.

Child 2:   I hate the salt. I wish I didn't have to take baths and wash my hair in salt water. My skin and clothes are itchy with salt.

Child 3:   What I hate most is the food. I'm so sick of dried beef, dried fish, and salt pork. And the biscuits are hard as rocks.

Child 4:   Don't forget the awful vegetables—parsnips and turnips.

Child 5:   I don't want to go to America. It's scary going to a new place. I already miss my friends.

Narrator 1:   The Pilgrims did have a lot to complain about. The *Mayflower* was a cargo ship. There was barely enough room for the 102 passengers and the 30 crew members.

Narrator 2:   During the trip, one of the beams that held the ship together cracked. Everyone had to help hold the beam while the ship's carpenter used a giant iron screw to put it back together.

Narrator 3:   And when there was no wind, the boat came to a standstill.

Child 1:   Yesterday, a baby boy was born. They named him Oceanus because he was born on the ocean.

Child 2:   He's lucky. He'll live in America and never know what it's like to worry about being arrested and going to prison.

Child 3:   My father says that in America we can make our own laws.

Child 4:   And we can worship God in our own way.

Child 5:   Then all the hardships will be worth it because we'll be free.

Child 1:   Do you think the native children will be friendly?

THE PILGRIM STORY

Act II
Cape Cod Bay
November 21, 1620

Characters
2 Crewmen
4 Narrators

Crewman 1: I can't believe it! After 65 days at sea, we've finally reached America!

Crewman 2: Now the Pilgrims can build their homes and we can sail back to England.

Narrator 1: But the Pilgrims' troubles were not over. The captain had made an error in navigation. Instead of landing in Virginia, the Pilgrims found themselves in New England.

Narrator 2: It was too cold to sail back to England. The crew planned to stay over until spring.

Narrator 3: Everyone had to stay on the ship until a permanent settlement was built.

Narrator 4: While still on board ship, the Pilgrims wrote the Mayflower Compact, the laws for the colony.

Narrator 1: In England, the king made the laws and the people had to obey them.

Narrator 2: In America, the Pilgrims made their own laws.

Narrator 3: After exploring the coastline, the Pilgrims anchored in Plymouth Harbor on December 26.

Narrator 4: They built sturdy houses out of lumber from nearby forests to shut out the harsh winter weather.

THE PILGRIM STORY

Act III
Plymouth Colony
Spring and Fall 1621

Characters
Squanto   3 Pilgrims
Samoset   5 Narrators

Pilgrim 1: This past winter was very cold and many people died. Food is running low, and there is still the threat of the natives.

Pilgrim 2: Look! Here come two natives!

Samoset: Welcome, Englishmen.

Pilgrim 3: Who are you? How do you know our language?

Samoset: My name is Samoset. I learned English from men who came to trade and fish near my village. This is Squanto.

Squanto: I can speak English. I will show you how to plant corn, beans, and pumpkins. I know the best way to fish and hunt. I will teach you.

Narrator 1: The Pilgrims and the natives became friends.

Narrator 2: When a young Pilgrim got lost in the woods, it was the natives who found him.

Narrator 3: When the Pilgrims learned that another tribe was planning to attack the Wampanoags, the Pilgrims gave them warning.

Narrator 4: When the chief got sick, the Pilgrims saved his life.

Narrator 5: The summer passed quickly. The harvest in November was good.

Pilgrim 1: We have been blessed in America. The Wampanoags are our friends. And the harvest has done well.

Pilgrim 2: Let's celebrate what God has given us with a feast of goose, duck, venison, vegetables, and cornbread!

Pilgrim 3: We can have contests and play games, too!

Pilgrim 1: What a great idea! And since the Wampanoags helped make this possible, we'll invite them.

Narrator 5: And that's just what they did.

Everyone: When the Pilgrims came to America, they wanted to be free. They had so much to be thankful for, and so do we!

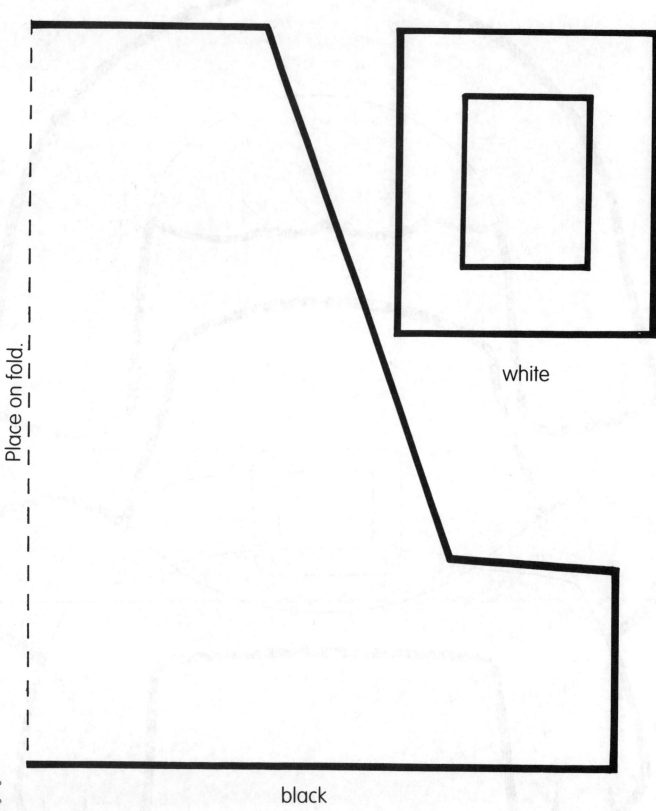

white

black

Place on fold.

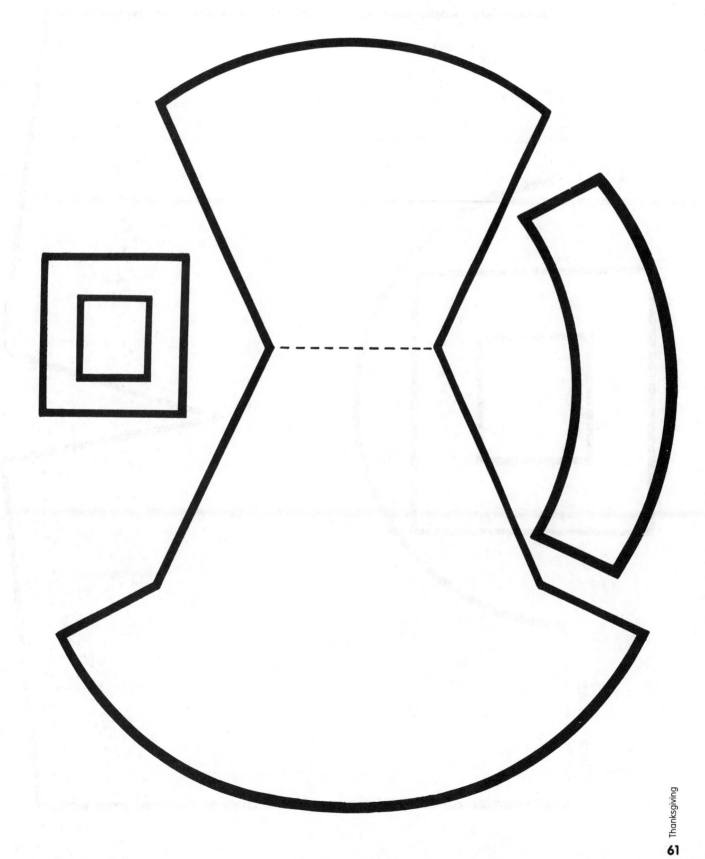

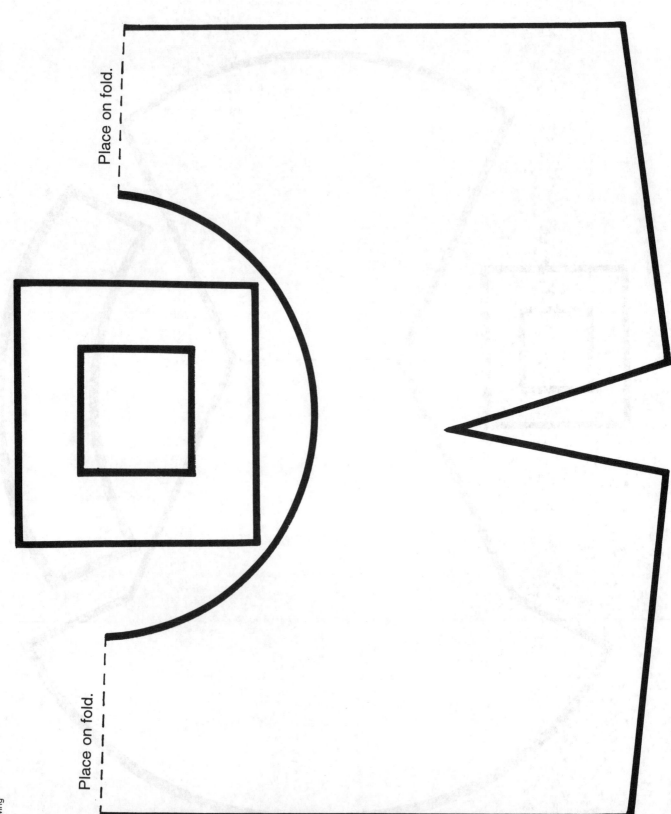

Place on fold.

Place on fold.

SQUANTO DAY

Squanto was a Patuxet Native American who helped the Pilgrims survive at Plymouth Colony. He served as an interpreter between the Pilgrims and the Wampanoag tribe, and he showed the Pilgrims how to plant corn and hunt and fish. Your students can pay tribute to his contributions with the following activities.

LITERATURE LINKS

The First Thanksgiving
by Jean Craighead George

Squanto and the First Thanksgiving
by Teresa N. Celsi and Pam Johnson

Squanto and the First Thanksgiving
by Joyce K. Kessel

Squanto, Friend of the Pilgrims
by Clyde R. Bulla

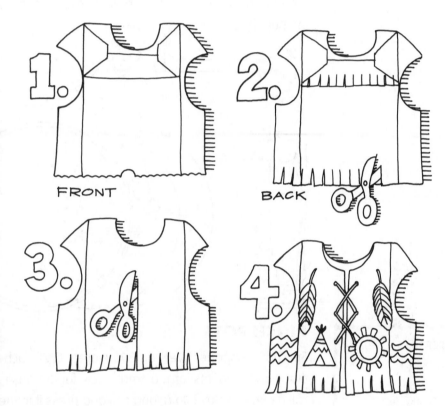

PAPER-SACK VESTS

Have students push out the sides of a paper grocery sack and lay it flat. Invite students to use the half-circle to trace and cut out two armholes and a neck hole. Staple the flap to the back of the sack. Invite students to cut fringe along the bottom of the sack and along the flap on the back of the vest. Have students turn the sack to the front side and cut a straight line (cutting through the top layer only) from the bottom of the sack to the neck hole. Help students hole-punch along each side of the opening on the front of the vest. Invite students to lace yarn through each set of holes. Have students use art supplies to decorate their vest with Native American designs.

MATERIALS

▲ brown paper grocery sacks
▲ 6" (15 cm) circle (cut in half)
▲ scissors
▲ stapler
▲ art supplies (crayons, markers, paint/paint-brushes, beads, feathers, ribbon, colored pasta, yarn, etc.)
▲ tape

HOOP GAMES

MATERIALS
▲ hula hoops
▲ beanbags

Native American villages often had a central area where men and boys gathered to compete in games of agility and endurance. Some tribes played a game in which players tried to hit a rolling hoop with a spear. To play a tamer version, divide your class into groups of three. Have two students in each group roll a hula hoop back and forth between them. Ask the third student to try to throw a beanbag through the hoop while standing three feet (1 m) away. When the student succeeds, he or she can trade places with the student who launched the hula hoop.

PINCH POTS

MATERIALS
▲ newspaper
▲ clay
▲ bowls of water
▲ paper clips or plastic knives
▲ paint/paintbrushes
▲ candy corn
▲ paper

Spread newspaper over your work area. Give each student a plum-size ball of clay. Have students form a small circle for the base of a pot. Then have students roll a piece of clay into a long coil and press it to the circle base. Invite students to continue rolling clay coils and wind them around the circle until a pot is formed. Have students dip their fingers in water and smooth the sides of the pot with their wet fingers. Invite students to use a paper clip or plastic knife to carve Native American designs or symbols on the sides of the pot. Let the clay pots air-dry overnight. Students can paint the pots after the clay is completely dry. Students can fill their pots with candy corn and messages telling family members why they are thankful for them.

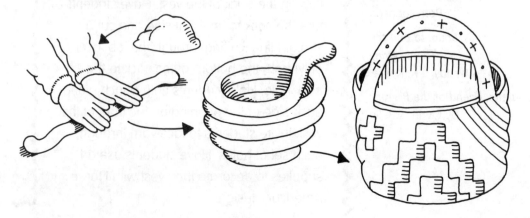

CORN ON THE COB DAY

Squanto taught the Pilgrims how to grow corn by putting a fish in a small hill of soil with the corn seed. The fish supplied the corn with food. Corn played an important role in the survival of the Pilgrims. This golden grain has been the staff of life for thousands of years. Enjoy a harvest of a-maize-ing activities with Corn on the Cob Day.

CORN HUSK DOLLS

Soak corn husks in a bucket of water until they are soft. Drain the water but keep the corn husks damp. Have each student layer five corn husks and roll another corn husk into a tight ball to create a head. Have students place the head in the center of the layered corn husks and fold the husks in half over the head. Ask students to tie a piece of string under the ball to make a neck. Have students roll one corn husk along its width to make arms and tie a string to each end. Invite students to slide the arms through the middle of the folded corn husks, just under the neck. Have students tie a piece of string below the arms to make a waist. Students can give their corn husk doll pants by cutting the middle of the loose corn husks, stopping about an inch (2.5 cm) below the waist. Then they can use string to tie the bottom of each leg. Invite students to decorate the faces with fine-tip markers. Have students glue on corn silk or yarn for hair and cut out clothing from fabric scraps or construction paper.

MATERIALS
▲ corn husks
▲ bucket of water
▲ string or twine
▲ scissors
▲ paper towels
▲ fine-tip markers
▲ corn silk or yarn
▲ fabric scraps or
   construction paper

MATERIALS
- ▲ yellow, orange, and brown tempera paint
- ▲ paper plates
- ▲ construction paper
- ▲ dried corn husks

CORNY ART

Pour paint on paper plates for students to share. Have students dip a finger in the paint and press it onto construction paper to print corn kernels. Ask students to keep using the same finger without washing it so the colors will blend and resemble Indian corn. Have students press the paint spots in the shape of an ear of corn. When the paint dries, invite students to glue corn husks on their paper so the artwork looks like a real ear of Indian corn.

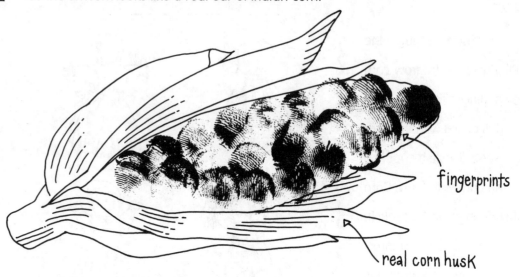

fingerprints

real corn husk

NATIVE AMERICAN CORN BELTS

MATERIALS
- ▲ fall-colored tempera paint
- ▲ paper plates
- ▲ newspaper
- ▲ uncooked ears of corn
- ▲ plastic corncob holders
- ▲ fabric strips

NATIVE AMERICAN CORN BELTS

Pour fall-colored paint on separate paper plates. Cover the work area with newspaper. Break uncooked ears of corn into 2"–4" (5 cm–10 cm) lengths. Firmly attach plastic corncob holders to the ends. Place one or two corncobs on each plate. Divide the class into small groups to share the paint. Have students roll the corn in the paint and then roll it on fabric strips to make Native American belts. Invite students to overlap patterns and hues. Remind students not to dip the same corn in more than one paint color. When belts dry, invite students to wear their festive belts home.

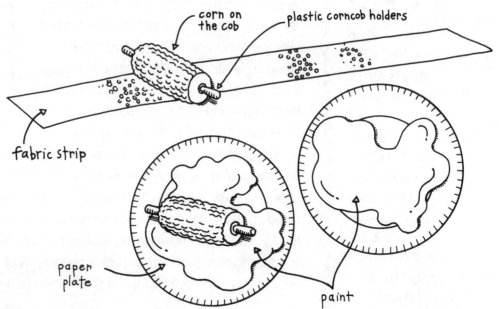

corn on the cob

plastic corncob holders

fabric strip

paper plate

paint

HIBERNATION DAY

Lizards, frogs, toads, snakes, bats, ground squirrels, hamsters, and hedgehogs hibernate. Their body temperature drops and their breathing and heart rate slow down so they can survive cold winters more easily when food is scarce. Highlight hibernating and deep-sleeping animals with the following activities—they'll keep your students from snoozing!

LITERATURE LINKS

Bernard Bear's Amazing Adventure
by Hans De Beer

Every Autumn Comes the Bear
by Jim Arnosky

How Do Bears Sleep?
by E. J. Bird

Possum's Harvest Moon
by Anne Hunter

Time to Sleep
by Denise Fleming

Wake Me in Spring
by James Preller

"BEARLY" SLEEPING MURAL

Divide the class into small groups and have each group decorate a hibernating or dormant animal in its home, such as a bear in a cave, a mole in a hole, a squirrel in a tree, or a badger in a hole. Hibernators include reptiles, amphibians, and insects (all cold-blooded creatures), plus a handful of mammals including the woodchuck, brown bat, and jumping mouse. Animals that are merely dormant include the chipmunk, raccoon, skunk, and bear. They are inactive and their metabolisms are slowed, but it is not uncommon for them to be roused even in winter to eat some food, when the weather is pleasant. Have students cut out their animal in its home and attach it to a bulletin board titled *Shh... Look Who's Hibernating!* Add fiberfill "snow" to the edges of the bulletin board. Invite students to label hibernating and dormant animals.

MATERIALS
▲ butcher paper
▲ construction paper
▲ paint/paintbrushes
▲ scissors
▲ fiberfill

HIBERNATING READ-IN

Plan a day for all students to bring to school sleeping bags or blankets, pillows, favorite books, and snacks. Invite students to use chairs to make cozy dens to "hibernate" during the day. Students can spend a quiet, restful day reading, snacking, and resting in their dens. Have students write about their day in journals.

HIBERNATING CAPS

Cut out four cap shapes from felt for each student using the Cap pattern. Invite students to use art supplies such as felt scraps, feathers, puffy pens, sequins, or buttons, to decorate their caps. Help students glue their caps together to fit their head. Have students wrap yarn around a small book until the yarn is thick. Help students pull the yarn off the book, tie a piece of yarn around the yarn bundle, and cut the ends of the yarn to create a pom-pom. Invite students to glue their pom-pom to the end of their cap. Have students wear their hibernating caps during story time.

CAP

ARTHUR DAY

He's smart.

D. W. is confident.

She likes to know everything about Arthur.

Arthur is a good friend.

He likes to joke with his sister.

He's a big brother.

November 27

Set up an Arthur reading corner in your classroom to celebrate Marc Brown's birthday. Gather Arthur props in a basket. Display the books and basket with stuffed animals and throw pillows.

LITERATURE LINKS

Books by Marc Brown

Arthur Babysits

Arthur Goes to Camp

Arthur Writes a Story

Arthur's Baby

Arthur's Birthday

Arthur's Chicken Pox

Arthur's Eyes

Arthur's First Sleepover

Arthur's New Puppy

Arthur's Nose

Arthur's Pet Business

Arthur's Thanksgiving

ANIMATED ARTHURS

After reading some of the Arthur books, ask students to name some of the main characters and their traits. Divide the class into small groups, and assign each group a character to create. Have the group choose someone to trace on butcher paper for the character's body. Ask students to work cooperatively to paint the butcher paper to resemble the character. Have each group describe the character's personality on sentence strips. Display the Arthur characters around the room.

MATERIALS
▲ Arthur books
▲ butcher paper
▲ markers
▲ paint/paintbrushes
▲ sentence strips

WHO AM I?

MATERIALS
▲ slips of paper
▲ basket
▲ chair

Write names of characters from the Arthur stories on slips of paper and place them in a basket. Choose one student at a time to pick a name and "become" that character. This person will sit in a chair in front of the room. The rest of the class may ask the person yes-no questions to try to figure out who he or she is. Select a volunteer to record all the information learned by the answers. Allow students to ask up to ten questions. The person who figures out the character gets to pick a name and sit in the chair next. If no one can figure out who the character is, the "character" gets to choose the next person to sit in the "character chair."

CLASS ARTHUR STORY

MATERIALS
▲ Arthur books
▲ chart paper
▲ construction paper
▲ crayons or markers

Read several Arthur books. Discuss common elements of Arthur stories. Begin by listing on chart paper the characters, setting, problem, and solution for the story. Then create a story plan. Invite students to choose their own setting, problem, and solution for an original Arthur story. Have students illustrate the story. Invite students to hide their names in the illustrations, as Marc Brown does in all of his books.

characters	setting	problem	solution
Arthur D.W. Brain Francine Muffy Buster	Skating rink	Arthur can't skate well and wants to give up.	He makes a goal after a lot of practice.

Arthur Plays Hockey
by Mr. Kupp's class

QUILT DAY

Cold winter days and nights make quilts a cozy topic for November. Invite your students to snuggle up with these cuddly quilt activities.

LITERATURE LINKS

Eight Hands Round: A Patchwork Alphabet by Ann W. Paul

The Josefina Story Quilt by Eleanor Coerr

The Keeping Quilt by Patricia Polacco

No Dragons on My Quilt by Jean Ray Laury

The Patchwork Lady by Mary K. Whittington

The Patchwork Quilt by Valerie Flournoy

The Quilt by Ann Jonas

The Quilt Story by Tony Johnston

The Seasons Sewn: A Year in Patchwork by Ann W. Paul

BATIK QUILT

Cut a white sheet into 6"–8" (15 cm–20 cm) squares, one per student. Heat wax in a slow cooker for about an hour. Invite students to draw a picture on a white cotton square using a permanent black marker. Have students use an old paintbrush dipped in the melted wax to paint the areas on their square they want to stay white. (Remind students of safety precautions when using hot wax, and supervise them carefully.) Have students wear rubber gloves and smocks. Students can dip their square in a bucket of water mixed with a light color of batik dye or food coloring and let their square dry. Invite students to paint with the melted wax over the areas they want to stay the light color and then dip their square into a darker color. Let the squares dry. As an alternative method, instead of dipping the squares into buckets of color, students can use a paintbrush to add color to the squares after applying the wax. Display the colorful batik quilt pieces individually or together on a bulletin board or wall.

MATERIALS

▲ white sheet
▲ scissors
▲ wax
▲ slow cooker
▲ permanent black markers
▲ paintbrushes
▲ batik dye, clothing dye, or food coloring
▲ buckets of water
▲ rubber gloves
▲ smocks

STORY QUILT

MATERIALS

▲ construction-paper squares
▲ chart paper
▲ crayons or markers
▲ glue
▲ butcher paper

Explain to students that quilts can be used to tell stories or historical events through the artwork. Choose a story or an historical event to portray through illustrations. For example, have students describe the first Thanksgiving in their own words, citing as many facts as they can. Record the facts on chart paper. Invite students to work with a partner to illustrate on a construction-paper square one historic fact from the chart paper. Ask students to sequence the illustrations in a time-line fashion and glue their illustrations to a butcher-paper background. Invite students to retell the story within the quilt.

Pilgrims were unhappy they could not practice their religion.

They left Holland for England.

They wanted more freedom to worship God. They left for America.

The voyage was rough. A baby was born, Oceanus.

SYMMETRICAL QUILT

MATERIALS

▲ 8" (20 cm) black construction-paper squares
▲ Quilt reproducible (page 74)
▲ crayons or markers
▲ hole punch
▲ yarn

Have students fold a black construction-paper square using the Quilt reproducible for a pattern. Discuss symmetry. Have students draw patterns or geometric shapes to create a symmetrical design on their square. Help students hole-punch two holes on each side of the square. Connect the squares by tying small pieces of yarn through the holes. Hang the quilt on a wall for a beautiful display.

QUILT

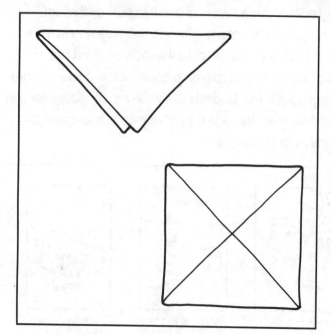

1. Fold a square along both diagonals.

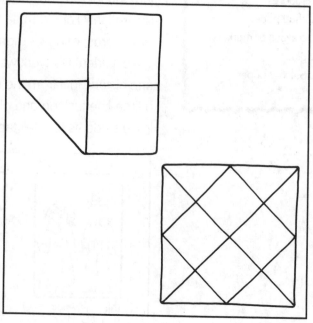

2. Fold each corner to the center.

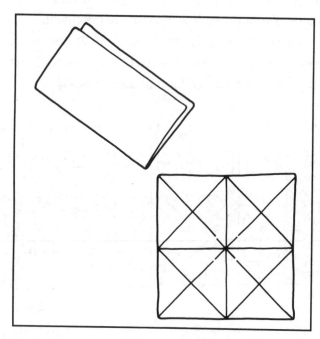

3. Fold in half both ways.

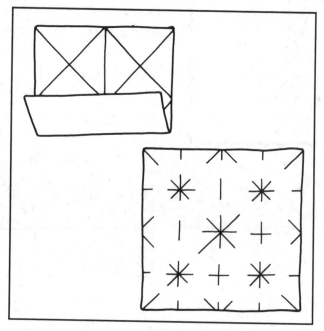

4. Fold each edge to the center. Decorate your quilt square.

November © 1998 Creative Teaching Press

MARVELOUS MAPS DAY

The third week in November is National Geography Awareness Week. Celebrate geography with Marvelous Maps Day. Students are sure to "find their way" with the following activities.

ladybug · bird chirping · red leaf · blue car · horn · ants · white fence · red door · snail · cat · yellow flower · barking dog

MAP WALK

Read aloud *Rosie's Walk* and discuss how Rosie was not very observant on her walk. List around the edge of a paper items students might see or hear on a walk around the neighborhood or school grounds, such as a bird, snail, bus, dandelion, and barking dog. Give each student a copy of the list. Tell students that to go on a walk they must be quiet, listen to all the sounds, and follow your directions to be more observant than Rosie. When students see or hear one of the items on the list, have them make a tear in the edge of the paper next to that item. Discuss how observant students were during their walk and how well they followed directions.

MATERIALS
▲ *Rosie's Walk*
by Pat Hutchins
▲ paper

MATERIALS

▲ heavy cardboard or wood
▲ 1 cup (250 ml) flour
▲ ¼ cup (50 ml) salt
▲ ⅓ cup (75 ml) water
▲ large bowl
▲ spoon
▲ paint/paintbrushes

RELIEF MAPS

Invite students to make a model of one of the earth's physical features, such as a mountain, volcano, or fjord. Have students use heavy cardboard or a piece of wood as a base. Make modeling clay by combining the flour, salt, and water in a large bowl. Invite students to knead or press the clay using their fingers. Have students shape the clay on their base and paint a map when the clay dries.

MATERIALS

▲ *Can You Read a Map?* CTP Learn to Read Series
▲ assorted fairy tales
▲ large construction paper
▲ crayons

FAIRY TALE MAPS

Read aloud *Can You Read a Map?* and review the settings for several well-known fairy tales. In each story, discuss where the characters are first, next, and last. (These places will become the key components for a map.) Have students select one of the fairy tales and ask them to draw a map to show where the characters went during the story. Ask students to include paths between the places and label the landmarks.

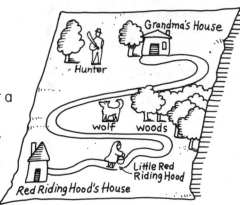

MATERIALS

▲ school map
▲ bright-colored paper
▲ ribbon
▲ treasure (treats)

TREASURE HUNT

In advance, create a legend on your school map and draw a star at your classroom. Make copies of the map and prepare clues on bright-colored paper for a treasure hunt. Roll the clues like scrolls and tie them with ribbon. Place the first clue next to the school map. The morning of the hunt, hide all the clues around the school in specific locations. When students arrive, tell them about the map you found. Pass out a map to each student. Read the first clue. Invite students to follow the map to find the next location revealed in the clue and continue following the clues and reading the map until they reach the treasure, which can be a tasty treat in the principal's office.

MY GEOGRAPHY BOOK

Have students color, cut out, and staple together the Geography Book pages. After students read the book, show the geographic features on a map.

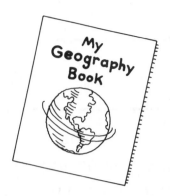

DIRECT CONNECTIONS

Label classroom walls with cardinal and intermediate directions. Call out a direction, and have students point to the wall with that direction. Pass out a U.S. map to each student. Have students place counters on each state you name. Ask students to give directions of states in relation to other states, such as *This state is north of Texas.* Have students place a counter on a given state and then give directions such as *Move your counter three states east and one state north.*

HOW FAR IS THAT?

Write the names of major cities on construction-paper triangles and tape the triangles to dowels or sticks to make pennants. Take the pennants, a U.S. map, and your students outdoors to a large open space. Have students locate the key on the map and explain to them that 1" (2.5 cm) will equal one pace on the ground. Invite students to make a large-scale ground map to help them envision large distances. Help students count out the paces to mark each of the four map corners. Invite students to stand at each corner of the map. Next, have students find their hometown and place the paper map on the equivalent location on the ground map. Have students measure the distance from their town to a major city on the paper map and then translate that distance into paces. Have one student hold one end of string on the hometown and another student extend the string to the major city on the ground map. Invite a student to place a pennant on that spot. Have students flag other cities in the same manner until all the major cities are marked. Ask students some basic geography questions such as *Would it be closer to visit Dallas, Texas or St. Louis, Missouri?* or *Would it take longer to drive to Boston, Massachusetts or Seattle, Washington?*

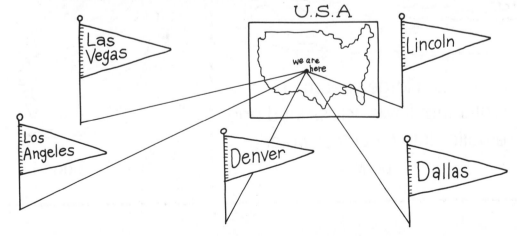

GEOGRAPHY BOOK

page 3
An island is an area of land completely surrounded by water.

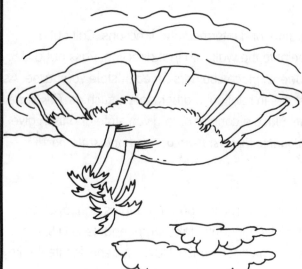

page 2
A peninsula is an area of land with water on three sides.

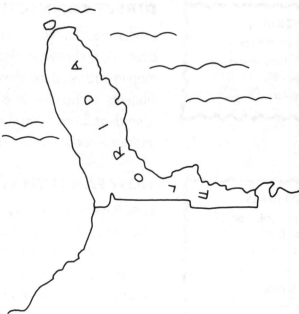

A river is a large stream of water that flows across land and empties into a body of water.

page 4

My Geography Book

page 1

GEOGRAPHY BOOK

November © 1998 Creative Teaching Press

A valley is a low area between mountains or hills.
page 7

A bay is a small body of water that cuts into land.
page 6

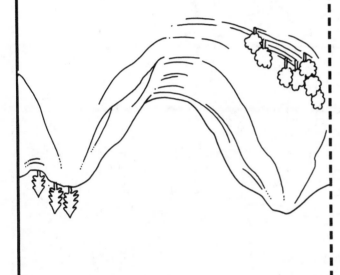

A mountain is a high landform on the earth's surface.
page 8

A lake is a body of water completely surrounded by land.
page 5

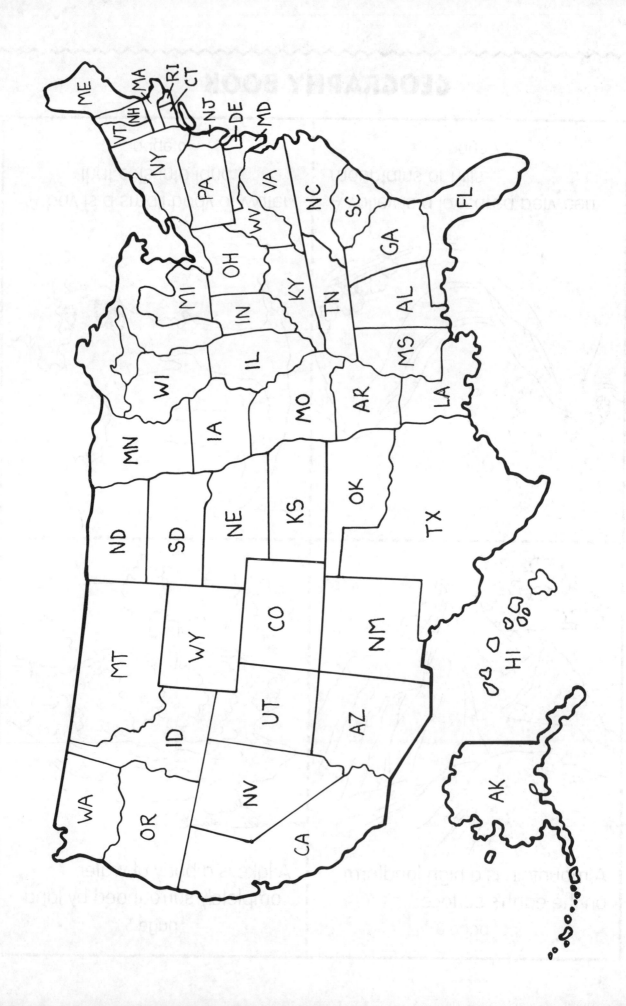

AIRPLANE DAY

November marks Aviation History Month, an ideal time to discuss the wonders and science of flight. Students will get off to a flying start with these spectacular activities!

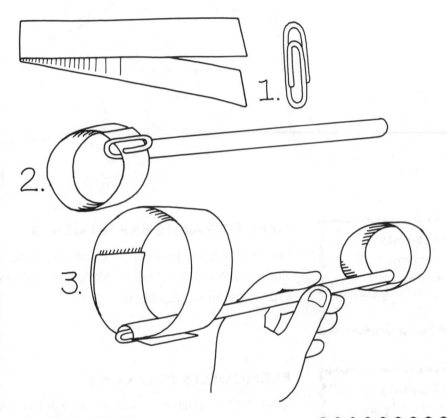

1.

2.

3.

LITERATURE LINKS

The Airplane Alphabet Book
by Jerry Pallotta

*The Berenstain Bears Fly-It!:
Up, Up and Away*
by Stan and Jan Berenstain

*Flight: The Journey
of Charles Lindbergh*
by Robert Burleigh

Flying by Gail Gibbons

The Glorious Flight
by Alice and Martin Provensen

I Fly
by Anne F. Rockwell

EASY GLIDERS

Have students put a paper clip into each end of a straw with the smaller loop of the paper clip on the outside. Have students align the paper-clip loops so they point toward each other. Have students fold the narrower paper strip in half and then make it into a loop with the ends overlapping. Help students attach the paper loop at the overlap to one of the paper clips and make a loop from the wide paper strip in a similar manner and attach it to the other paper clip. Ask students to make sure the two paper loops are aligned, while they hold the straw in the center with the smaller loop facing forward. Invite students to give the glider a push forward and watch it fly.

MATERIALS
▲ paper clips
▲ drinking straws
▲ 1 ¹/₂" x 11" (4 cm x 28 cm) paper strips
▲ ³/₄" x 11" (2 cm x 28 cm) paper strips

MAKE A PARACHUTE

Cut plastic trash bags into 12" (30.5 cm) squares. Ask each student to poke a small hole near each corner of a plastic square. Have students tie a string at each of the holes; then have them tie the loose strings together with one knot about 2" (5 cm) from the ends. Help students tie the strings on a spool. Invite students to practice dropping the parachute from a high place. Record student observations about how the parachute falls when closed and what happens when it begins to open.

MATERIALS

▲ plastic trash bags
▲ 12" (30.5 cm) string
▲ pencils
▲ empty spools of thread

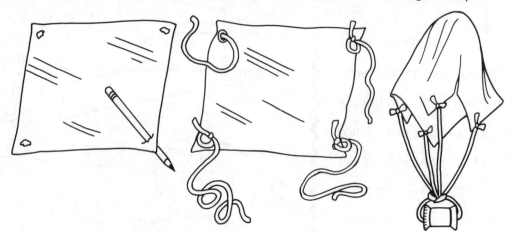

AERODYNAMIC EXPERIMENTS

Invite students to observe how an object's shape affects its movement. Give each student a copy of the Aerodynamics reproducible and have students conduct the experiment with scrap paper.

MATERIALS

▲ scrap paper
▲ Aerodynamics reproducible (page 83)

BERNOULLI'S PRINCIPLE

Have students push a thumbtack through the center of the tagboard square and place the tagboard on their table with the point of the thumbtack showing. (The thumbtack will keep the tagboard from slipping during the experiment.) Ask students to place one end of their spool over the point of the thumbtack and blow into the spool. As students blow, have them raise the spool. If they blow hard enough, the tagboard will be lifted.

Explain that by blowing through the spool, students are forcing air to move across the top of the tagboard. This moving air has less pressure, or force, than the air below the tagboard. The unequal pressure on either side of the tagboard creates a "lift."

MATERIALS

▲ 2" (5 cm) square tagboard
▲ thumbtacks
▲ empty spools of thread

AERODYNAMICS

Name _____

Shape of paper	What happened when you dropped it? (Circle the best answer.)
one flat sheet	It fell: fast slow It fell: straight down with a side-to-side motion It fell: always facing one direction with a spinning motion
wadded into a ball	It fell: fast slow It fell: straight down with a side-to-side motion It fell: always facing one direction with a spinning motion
fringed along the edges	It fell: fast slow It fell: straight down with a side-to-side motion It fell: always facing one direction with a spinning motion
folded like a fan	It fell: fast slow It fell: straight down with a side-to-side motion It fell: always facing one direction with a spinning motion
your shape	It fell: fast slow It fell: straight down with a side-to-side motion It fell: always facing one direction with a spinning motion

PEANUT BUTTER DAY

With more vitamins than beef liver, more carbohydrates than potatoes, and packed full of protein, the peanut is a powerhouse of energy. Peanut butter is an American favorite. The average American will eat three pounds of peanut butter this year! Your students will love these peanut butter projects planned for National Peanut Butter Lover's Month.

LITERATURE LINKS

Make Me a Peanut Butter Sandwich and a Glass of Milk by Ken Robbins

Peanut Butter and Bologna Sandwiches by Pamm Jenkins

Peanut Butter and Jelly by Nadine Westcott

Peanut Butter (How It's Made) by Arlene Erlbach

Where the Sidewalk Ends by Shel Silverstein

PEANUT, PEANUT BUTTER

Read *Peanut Butter and Jelly* aloud. Chant the rhyme, having half the class chant *Peanut, peanut butter,* and the other half whisper in chorus *Jelly, jelly* as the story is read again. Set up several stations for making peanut butter and jelly sandwiches. Have students use the terms *first, next, then,* and *last* to discuss the steps needed to make the sandwiches. Assign students to make sandwiches. While they are eating, read the poem, "Peanut Butter Sandwich."

MATERIALS
- ▲ *Peanut Butter and Jelly* by Nadine Westcott
- ▲ bread slices
- ▲ peanut butter
- ▲ jelly (assorted flavors)
- ▲ paper plates
- ▲ plastic knives
- ▲ napkins
- ▲ "Peanut Butter Sandwich" from *Where the Sidewalk Ends* by Shel Silverstein

PEANUT BUTTER PERIMETER

MATERIALS

▲ peanut butter
▲ crackers
▲ raisins
▲ plastic knives
▲ paper plates

Give each student a cracker, plastic knife and a handful of raisins. Place a paper plate with peanut butter on it on desks for students to share. Explain to students that the perimeter is the distance around an object. Ask students to predict how many raisins it will take to go around the outside of their cracker. Then invite students to spread peanut butter on their cracker and measure the perimeter of it using the raisins. Students can also measure the area by counting how many raisins fit on the cracker. Discuss the results. Eat and enjoy!

PEANUT BUTTER IS BEST

MATERIALS

▲ construction paper
▲ scissors
▲ crayons or markers

Cut out peanut shapes from construction paper. Ask students what they like best to eat with peanut butter. Have students complete and illustrate on construction paper the poem *At home, what does (student's name) request? He/she says "Peanut butter and _____ are the best."*

DINOSAUR DAY

Match your students' enthusiasm for these Mesozoic monsters with some facinating fun. Students will really "dig" unearthing dinosaurs during a blockbuster learning experience on Dinosaur Day. It's dino-mite!

LITERATURE LINKS

Bones, Bones, Dinosaur Bones
by Byron Barton

Danny and the Dinosaur
by Syd Hoff

Digging Up Dinosaurs by Aliki

Dinamation's Dinosaurs Alive
by Dinamation
International Corporation

Dinosaurs by Gail Gibbons

Dinosaurs Dancing
CTP Learn to Read Series

Patrick's Dinosaurs
by Carol Carrick

Tyrannosaurus Was a Beast
by Jack Prelutsky

*Whatever Happened
to the Dinosaurs?*
by Bernard Most

CHIP AWAY!

A week in advance, wrap individual plastic dinosaurs in small balls of clay and let them dry. Before students arrive to class on Dinosaur Day, turn over a few desks, leave a few big dinosaur footprints around the room, and hide the balls of clay in a sandbox or around your classroom. When students arrive, tell them that it looks like a dinosaur visited their classroom. Read aloud *Digging Up Dinosaurs* and teach students the song "Dinosaur Dig." Invite them to become paleontologists and go on a dinosaur dig. When the paleontologists find the balls of clay, give them nails and old toothbrushes. Invite students to excavate their dinosaurs. Carefully supervise students while they use nails. Invite students to identify their dinosaurs and write facts about them.

MATERIALS

- ▲ clay
- ▲ small, plastic dinosaurs
- ▲ *Digging Up Dinosaurs* by Aliki
- ▲ Dinosaur Dig (page 88)
- ▲ large nails
- ▲ old toothbrushes
- ▲ writing paper

DINOSAUR HATS

MATERIALS

▲ Dinosaur Hat reproducible (page 89)
▲ crayons or markers
▲ scissors
▲ sentence strips
▲ glue
▲ stapler
▲ audiocassette of "Dinosaurs Dancing" by Steven Traugh from *Music & Movement in the Classroom* (CTP)
▲ audiocassette player

Have students color and cut out the Dinosaur Hat reproducible. Invite students to glue it to the center of a sentence strip. Staple the ends of each strip together to fit each student's head. Invite students to wear their dinosaur hats while they dance to the song "Dinosaurs Dancing."

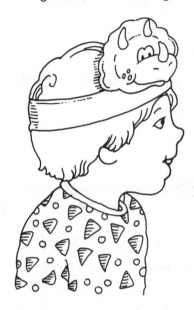
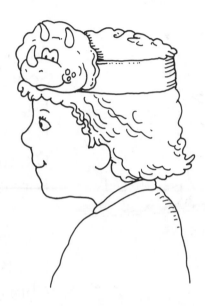

DINOSAUR TAKE-HOME BAG

MATERIALS

▲ canvas bag
▲ plastic dinosaurs
▲ dinosaur books
▲ family letter (page 90)

HOME ACTIVITY

Send home with each student a canvas bag with plastic dinosaurs, dinosaur books, and a copy of the family letter inside. Have students take turns taking the bag home and doing the activities with their family members.

DINOSAUR DIG

(to the tune of: "Dixie")

I'm going on a dinosaur dig,
Searching for eggs that are really big.
Dig away,
Dig away,
Dig away,
For some eggs.

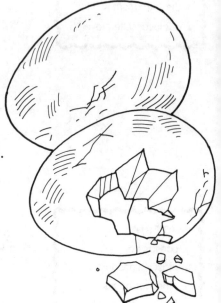

See the dinosaur eggs I found.
Hidden away deep in the ground.
Chip away,
Chip away,
Chip away,
At the eggs.

I discovered a baby dinosaur,
That may have been a carnivore.
In the egg,
In the egg,
In the egg,
That I found.

I'm a paleontologist,
Learning how they did exist,
When I dig,
And I dig,
And I dig,
For dinosaurs.

Dear Family,

To celebrate Dinosaur Day, please help me complete the following activities.

1. Read and discuss the dinosaur books with me.

2. Help me sort the plastic dinosaurs by different categories, such as meat- and plant-eaters, big and little, or spikes and no spikes.

Name_____

This is a drawing of my favorite dinosaur.

My favorite dinosaur is _____ because

_____

_____

NOVEMBER

SUNDAY	MONDAY	TUESDAY	WEDNESDAY	THURSDAY	FRIDAY	SATURDAY

November © 1998 Creative Teaching Press

Pilgrim Border

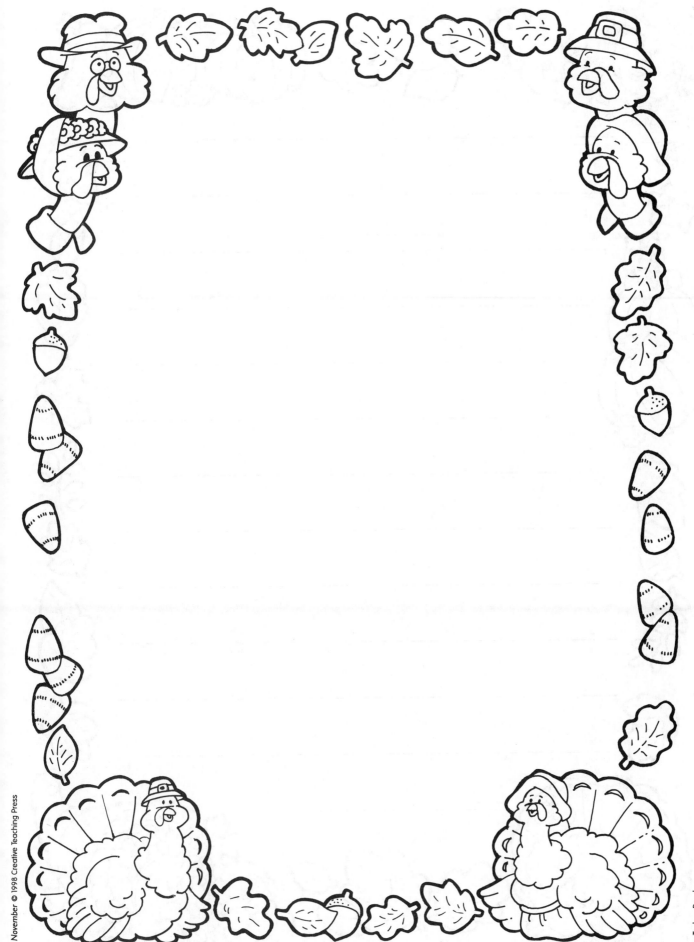

November News

NOVEMBER